SWITZERLAND
The MONOCLE Handbook

MONOCLE

First published in the United Kingdom in 2025
by MONOCLE and Thames & Hudson Ltd,
6–24 Britannia Street, London WC1X 9JD
thamesandhudson.com

First published in the United States of America in 2025
by MONOCLE and Thames & Hudson Inc,
500 Fifth Avenue, New York, New York, 10110
thamesandhudsonusa.com

MONOCLE is a trading name of Winkontent Limited

EU Authorised Representative: Interart S.A.R.L.
19 rue Charles Auray, 93500 Pantin, Paris, France
productsafety@thameshudson.co.uk
interart.fr

British Library Cataloguing-in-Publication Data
A catalogue record for this book is available from
The British Library
Library of Congress Control Number: 2025934101
For more information, please visit *monocle.com*

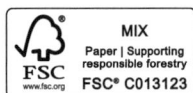

Edited by *Amy van den Berg*
Introduction by *Tyler Brûlé*

Designed by MONOCLE
Proofreading by MONOCLE
Typeset in *Plantin*

Printed in Italy by *Graphicom*
ISBN 978-0-500-96641-9
01

Cover images
Front cover (clockwise)
Badi Küssnacht by Yves Bachmann; ice rink at Suvretta
House by Fabrizio D'Aloisio;
Pavillon Le Corbusier by Lea Meienberg
Back cover (clockwise from top left)
Magdalena Bäckerei by Sabine Hess; Glacier Express
by Yves Bachmann; Montreux Jazz Festival by Marc
Ducrest; Cabane Mont Fort by Melody Sky

Switzerland

The MONOCLE Handbook

DISCOVER SWITZERLAND

PART 01

We travelled up mountains, careered down bobsleigh runs and ate a lot of good chocolate to scope out the very best this innovative nation has to offer. Over the following pages we'll take you to glittering belle époque hotels, sharply modern Alpine retreats and traditional hilltop guesthouses; meet dedicated artisans keeping skills alive and highly imaginative designers, architects and entrepreneurs; and, of course, visit the best places in the country to ski, swim and relax.

PUT DOWN ROOTS

PART 02

Fallen in love with Switzerland? Then it's time to extend your stay – maybe indefinitely.
In this chapter we show you the best places to open a business, introduce you to the
architects and designers who can help turn your dream into a reality and peek inside
some Swiss homes along the way. We also hear from bold entrepreneurs who
have already made the move.

ADDRESS BOOK

PART 03

Use this handy guide to plan your next trip. Here we present a list of our favourite
places to stay, eat, shop and visit, organised by region. Whether you're heading
to Andermatt or Zürich, we've got you covered.

Whether you're visiting for a weekend getaway or planning to stay for longer, *Switzerland: The Monocle Handbook* makes the perfect travel companion. What are you waiting for?

INTRODUCTION

———————————————————————————————

TYLER BRÛLÉ
Editorial director *&* chairman

This fifth edition in our handbook series is something of a homecoming as much of what's covered across these pages is in our own backyard. Since MONOCLE launched in 2007, Switzerland has been our official HQ and Zürich the hub for our varied pursuits. For the broader activities of our holding company and for me, the story goes even further back and it's for this reason that this might be our most personal volume to date.

From our favourite haunts near our HQ in Zürich's Seefeld and the best tables in the Engadine to locations to bathe in Geneva, our handbook is not only a collection of places to escape for a long weekend or check in for a month-long retreat but also an informed companion to help you contemplate a more permanent set-up in this perfectly formed Alpine nation.

In a volatile world, Switzerland continues to be a draw for people looking for an enhanced quality of life, security, stability and a point at the crossroads of Europe. At our café on Zürich's Dufourstrasse, our colleagues are often asked by visitors, "What's it really like to live in Switzerland?" Or, "How can I get a slice of this at some point in my life?" This edition aims to answer those questions and many more. If you don't find what you're looking for between these covers, then you can always swing by our HQ for a few additional tips. *Merci.* Enjoy.

MAPS

Modern Switzerland came together in 1848 after centuries of shifting alliances and a short but memorable visit from Napoleon. Don't let its modest size fool you. Top to bottom, it covers just 220km and it is only 348km across but it borders five countries and squeezes in a world of mountains, valleys and Alpine charm. Switzerland is made up of 26 cantons, each with its own flavour and strong sense of independence. What unites them is direct democracy and a shared love of punctual trains, hiking and cooling off in one of the country's 1,500 lakes. The Alps are the backbone of Switzerland, covering two-thirds of the country and shaping everything from the weather to how people get around. The Dufourspitze is the highest mountain but it has stiff competition from postcard stars such as the Matterhorn and Jungfraujoch, the location of the highest train station in Europe. With 48 peaks over 4,000 metres, Swiss life often revolves around these snowy giants. South of the Alps lies sunny Ticino, where things are more Italian. Head to Geneva and you'll find French flair, while some in remote Graubünden communities speak Latin-derived Romansh.

Eastern Switzerland: From ample farmland to Alpine peaks – one of the country's most diverse regions.

Zürich: Switzerland's hub of finance and culture.

Central Switzerland: Modernity meets tradition in the heart of the country.

Northwestern Switzerland: The mighty Rhine flows through lush farmland around the port city of Basel.

Espace Mittelland: The French-German polyglot "central plateau".

Arc Lémanique: The seat of French-speaking Switzerland to the north of Lake Geneva.

Ticino: Italian-speaking Switzerland, south of the Alps.

GERMANY

0   50   100
km

N

FRANCE

Basel 5
11
18
4
1
Baden
Baden
16
5
20
ZÜRICH
19 St Gallen
26
2   3
LIECHT.
AUSTRIA

BERNE 6
13
12 Lucerne
17
9
15 14
Davos

SWITZERLAND
22
10

Freiburg
7
Andermatt
St Moritz

24
Lausanne
Gstaad

8 GENEVA
Sion
21
Verbier
23
Zermatt
Lugano

FRANCE
ITALY

Swiss cantons

1.	Aargau	14.	Nidwalden
2.	Appenzell Ausserrhoden	15.	Obwalden
3.	Appenzell Innerrhoden	16.	Schaffhausen
4.	Basel-Landschaft	17.	Schwyz
5.	Basel-Stadt	18.	Solothurn
6.	Berne	19.	St Gallen
7.	Fribourg	20.	Thurgau
8.	Geneva	21.	Ticino
9.	Glarus	22.	Uri
10.	Graubünden	23.	Valais
11.	Jura	24.	Vaud
12.	Lucerne	25.	Zug
13.	Neuchâtel	26.	Zürich

NEED TO KNOW

We turn a spotlight on the nation's traditions and quirks, from its citizens' socially and environmentally responsible approach to civic duty and their mastery of various languages to their expertise in multiple methods of traversing snow-covered landscapes.

THE ALPINE SPIRIT
Mountains, adventure and tradition

Switzerland's mountainous landscapes define its identity. Whether skiing on world-class slopes in winter, hiking through Alpine meadows in summer or simply admiring iconic peaks such as the Matterhorn, the mountains are central to Switzerland's leisure and tourism. They are not just a playground for adventure but also a symbol of national pride and heritage. Beyond skiing and hiking, the Alps offer an incredible range of activities for every season. In winter, snowshoeing is a perfect way to explore peaceful, untouched landscapes away from the busy slopes, while tobogganing (*schlitteln*) down winding mountain tracks is an exhilarating experience. It's common to see young children who can barely stand skiing confidently in the *skischule* (ski school). In the warmer months, the mountains transform into a paradise for outdoor enthusiasts. Crystal-clear Alpine lakes invite visitors for a refreshing swim, while *via ferrata*s allow climbers to experience the thrill of exposed rock faces.

A MULTILINGUAL NATION
Allegra, grüezi, ciao and bonjour!

Switzerland has four official national languages – German, French, Italian and Romansh – meaning the country is unavoidably multilingual. Street signs are often in several languages and train announcements reflect the nation's linguistic diversity. Students learn at least one additional national language at school, ensuring easy communication across regions. Many Swiss residents also speak English fluently, as well as other lingua francas such as Spanish or Portuguese. Due to large expatriate communities and global connections, this tendency extends to many other languages too. In international settings, Swiss multilingualism enhances the nation's role as a mediator, cultural centre and global hub, with the majority of its people able to seamlessly switch between languages in professional and social contexts.

A STABLE AND SHARED PATH
Neutrality and empowered citizens

Switzerland's neutrality has kept it out of conflict since 1815, positioning it as a hub for peace and diplomacy. The country rarely takes sides in international disputes, preferring mediation and consensus-building over confrontation. Its hosting of numerous international organisations, including the United Nations in Geneva, reinforces Switzerland's reputation as a nation for dialogue and co-operation. The Swiss people also prefer to share power rather than dominate others. This is reflected in the country's unique system of direct democracy, in which citizens vote on national, cantonal and local issues multiple times a year. From deciding on taxation to environmental regulations, the Swiss population plays an active role in shaping the nation's laws.

SWISS CRAFTSMANSHIP
Watches that stand the test of time

Swiss watches are renowned for their precision, luxury and exceptional craftsmanship. Heritage brands such as Rolex, Vacheron Constantin, Omega and Patek Philippe have become global symbols of excellence, reflecting Switzerland's deep-rooted commitment to quality and innovation. The intricate skills behind Swiss watchmaking take years to master, with artisans undergoing decades of apprenticeship to meticulously refine their craft. But Switzerland's dedication to exactitude extends beyond watches. The country is also a leader in high-performance engineering: from cutting-edge medical technology and advanced surgical instruments to precision chocolate-making machinery and household tools. Whether it's a mechanical masterpiece passed down through generations or the reliability of a Swiss Army Knife, Switzerland's unrivalled devotion to craftsmanship ensures that quality never goes out of style.

THE TASTE OF SWITZERLAND
Tradition with a touch of modernity

From *rösti* in a chalet to a simple *cervelat* sausage grilled over an open fire, Swiss cuisine balances quality and craftsmanship. Cheese reigns supreme. Gruyère, emmental and appenzeller are more than just pantry ingredients: they are a gastronomy tradition rooted in the country's dairy-farming heritage. Chocolate has been perfected over generations, with heritage brands such as Cailler and Sprüngli setting global standards. Then there are the distinctly Swiss favourites: Ovomaltine, the tasty chocolate drink and bread spread, Rivella, the slightly mysterious, milk-derived drink that remains a national obsession, and muesli, a wholesome breakfast staple. Beyond nostalgia, Swiss cuisine is evolving. Michelin-starred chefs reinterpret classic Alpine dishes and farm-to-table movements champion local produce.

ENVIRONMENTAL AND SOCIETAL ORDER
Clean, green and sustainable

Switzerland is globally recognised for its cleanliness: streets, trains and public spaces are impeccably maintained and recycling is not just encouraged but expected. Public responsibility is key. Littering is rare and even remote hiking trails remain pristine thanks to a shared sense of environmental stewardship. Beyond recycling, sustainability is woven into daily life. Hydropower provides a major share of the country's energy and the extensive rail network operates largely on renewable electricity, making train travel an environmentally conscious and popular choice. Whether it's the structured waste system, sustainable urban planning or renewable energy use, Switzerland's commitment to ecological responsibility remains as precise as its renowned timekeeping.

HIGH QUALITY OF LIFE
Living well, but at a cost

Swiss cities frequently rank among the most liveable in the world, thanks to exceptional public services, safety and reliable infrastructure. Efficient public transport, clean streets and well-maintained public spaces contribute to an environment that feels both organised and inviting. Access to world-class education, high salaries and political stability further reinforce the country's reputation for excellence. However, this high standard of living comes at a price: Switzerland is one of the most expensive countries in the world, with high rental, grocery and healthcare prices. Mandatory health insurance alone is a major expense, while childcare and public transport are also costly. There is additional insurance for accident coverage, travel insurance and e-bikes, reflecting the Swiss preference for security and preparedness. But despite the expenses, the benefits of living in Switzerland remain undeniable. The balance between urban efficiency and access to pristine nature, combined with an emphasis on safety and innovation, ensures that the country continues to set the benchmark for a high quality of life.

PART 01

DISCOVER SWITZERLAND

Take a tour of the country's hospitality, shopping, culture and architecture scenes – plus the most uniquely Swiss experiences that it has to offer.

From exhilarating mountaintop redoubts to discreet luxury palaces and chic urban hideaways, Switzerland has much to teach the world about fine accommodation. Here is our pick of the best examples.

WHERE TO STAY

The fantastic tale of a mountain-village boy turned acclaimed hotelier with institutions spanning London, Paris and beyond still captures the imagination. César Ritz's ingenuity and personal approach are the founding pillars of the Swiss hospitality tradition. Though the building boom of the belle époque is never coming back, many grand hotels from the golden age still stand in their palatial splendour and offer impeccable service as they did more than a century ago. We will also introduce you to bright-eyed entrepreneurs who have spruced up historic villas and chalets, now ready for idyllic getaways. Whether you're in the mood for a bijou locale and enjoying a slice of living history, or visiting a new opening with a hip crowd, we have you covered. If you dare to venture beyond the well-known cities you'll find plenty of thoughtful hideouts in unexpected outposts. You might need a cable car or even snow shoes to reach some but you'll be rewarded with peerless views and excellent service.

THE EDIT

1 **Mountain hotels**
From quaint village inns to space-age modernist utopias, Swiss mountain hotels cover a wide range.

2 **Urban hotels**
Set in Switzerland's immaculate cityscapes, here is our selection of the country's best urban boltholes.

3 **The experts**
Four hospitality insiders give us their thoughts on the present and future of the country's hotel industry.

MOUNTAIN HOTEL
HOTEL OLDEN
Gstaad

The small-world feel of Hotel Olden belies its reputation as a *bon vivant* hangout in the 1970s, where locals would rub shoulders with celebrities. Built in 1690, it underwent multiple transformations until it turned into an elegant hospitality establishment in 1952. It is now owned by the family of Bernie Ecclestone. In the kitchen, Abruzzo-born chef Nico Lusi (*pictured, on left at top of stairs next to Ecclestone*) mixes Mediterranean and international recipes with southern-Italian accents, creating delights including homemade *gnocchi cacio e pepe* with truffle, and *penne alla vodka* with beef pastrami. *hotelolden.com*

Their way
Frank Sinatra's beer stein remains here as a relic of the hotel's glamorous heyday but the Swiss chalet-hotel doesn't flaunt its renown. Instead, guests (many of who return time and again) are addressed personally. "We like to think of ourselves as a club without the need for membership," says managing director Pierpaolo Gardella.

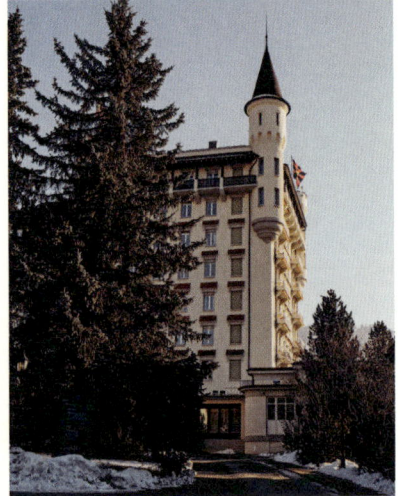

MOUNTAIN HOTEL
GSTAAD PALACE
Gstaad

Since Gstaad became accessible via the Bernois Railway in 1904, it has been hailed for its upscale hospitality. But few are aware of the role of the Gstaad Palace in writing this narrative. Gstaad's most iconic hotel was opened in 1913 by local teacher Robert Steffen, who noticed a demand for a luxury hotel from aristocratic travellers. In 1947 the Scherz family bought the Palace, later attracting the likes of Quentin Tarantino and Princess Diana. La Fromagerie restaurant serves decadent fondue and, come nightfall, guests let their hair down at the flamboyant in-house nightclub.
palace.ch

Rooms with a view
Owner Andrea Scherz – the third generation of his family to take the helm of the Gstaad Palace – recommends booking the penthouse for fairy tale-like scenes of the Wasserngrat, Wispiele and Eggli mountain ranges and a bird's-eye perspective of the snow-capped roofs below. "You'll feel like the king of Gstaad," he says.

MOUNTAIN HOTEL
LE CHALET LION ROUGE
Rougemont, Vaud

This beautiful 300-year-old farmhouse feels like something from a story book. Featuring classic Alpine details such as timber walls and carved balustrades, the spacious chalet has seven bedrooms in earthy tones with relaxed modern furnishings. Three salons with fireplaces provide refuges to unwind in, while the terrace offers views of Rougemont village from its 1,200-metre-high perch. Guests can enjoy French and Swiss wines alongside dishes prepared by a private chef. A fresh breakfast and local cheeses and eggs are available to fuel visitors for a day of hiking or skiing with an on-hand instructor. End the day with a Finnish sauna and a glass of something reviving on the terrace.
84rooms.com

MOUNTAIN HOTEL
THE OMNIA
Zermatt

The Omnia is nestled way up in the Alps. This modern take on a classic mountain lodge looks out to the Matterhorn and has a tunnel entrance from the street. "We're high above Zermatt, where the heavens meet the earth," says managing director Christian Eckert. The building, designed by Ali Tayar, features bay windows, fireplaces, elegant baths and classic USM modular furniture (*see page 190*), which contribute to a homely feel inside. Warmth also comes from the cuisine, which makes use of fresh, local produce, and a wellness centre that provides guests with the ultimate relaxation experience. *the-omnia.com*

MOUNTAIN HOTEL
CERVO
Zermatt

The Cervo's 54 rooms and suites are in chalets perched on the Sunnegga mountain with views of the Matterhorn. The hotel's chic version of Alpine luxury includes custom furniture, a multi-level stone hot pool and a glasshouse lounge perfect for catching the morning sun. Opened in 2009 by Daniel and Seraina Lauber, the hotel boasts a full-service spa and three restaurants, and is known for its après-ski: one of Zermatt's valley runs deposits skiers at the hotel. "We believe that people should be in motion, skiing, hiking, out exploring, then in the evening enjoying the best wines and food," says Cervo's founder and hotelier, Daniel F Lauber.
cervo.swiss

MOUNTAIN HOTEL
EXPERIMENTAL CHALET
Verbier

For Pierre-Charles Cros, co-owner of the Paris-based Experimental Group, the goal was to avoid Alpine clichés in the 39 highly styled rooms of this outpost of the company, so designer Fabrizio Casiraghi looked to the South Tyrol region for ideas. "The result is a very cosy but less déjà vu design – more stripped-back at first, yet appealing and relaxing," says Cros. There's plenty to enjoy after the pistes, such as the spa featuring an ice bath, sauna and a large Jacuzzi. Plus, with the Experimental Cocktail Club and Farm Club (a fixture of Verbier nightlife for more than 50 years), days here end well.
experimentalchalet.com

MOUNTAIN HOTEL
MICHELHAUS
Ernen, Valais

Once a neglected chalet, Michelhaus was transformed into a luxurious two-apartment retreat by Reto Holzer (*pictured*). Holzer bought the house in 2020 and now it welcomes visitors with 400-year-old floors, a stone hearth (complete with the coat of arms of the original owners, Christen and Frena Michel), plus antique milking stools, cowbells and *brocante* paintings. Other furnishings include Carl Hansen chairs and Mies van der Rohe's Barcelona daybed, and all beds are by Hästens. "I like the mix of old and new," says Holzer. "We want our guests to feel at home – relaxed, comfortable and welcomed." *michelhaus.ch*

MOUNTAIN HOTEL
SIX SENSES
Crans-Montana, Valais

Six Senses has brought its signature blend of wellness and design to the heart of the Swiss Alps. This ski-in, ski-out retreat swaps chalet style for bold but comforting architecture. The wellness spa features a striking pool that stretches into a brutalist-style courtyard of birch trees. The therapeutic offerings are both soothing and unabashedly cutting-edge, with facilities including a steam room, multiple saunas, a flotation pod and a yoga studio. Dining is equally impressive: Wild Cabin cooks up bold seasonal fare, while Byakko serves sushi in a slick après-ski setting.
sixsenses.com

DISCOVER SWITZERLAND | MOUNTAIN HOTELS

MOUNTAIN HOTEL
VILLA FLOR
S-chanf, Graubünden

Art and soul
Works by American painter Julian
Schnabel – who has been a guest – can
be discovered here, as can those of Swiss
photographer Albert Steiner and German
conceptual artist Karin Sander. Artist
Philipp Keel and designer Nathalie du
Pasquier (a founder of the Memphis
Group) are also friends of the house.

The Upper Engadine village of S-chanf sits at a height of
1,660 metres and is close to the Swiss National Park. It
is also known in art circles. Ladina Florineth, the owner
of the Villa Flor, has made sure of that. In 2009 she and
architect Christian Klainguti took on the classicist
patrician house from 1904 and revived it. "We had the
art nouveau paintings extensively restored, saved the
pine wall and ceiling panelling and polished the 100-year-
old stoves," says Florineth. She turned the seven rooms
into delightful retreats using family heirlooms, flea-market
finds and mid-century design classics. All are adorned with
artworks and serve as a gallery for the hostess's collection.
villaflor.ch

MOUNTAIN HOTEL
PIZ LINARD
Lavin, Graubünden

The Piz Linard – named after the highest peak of the Silvretta, which is not far from Lavin – has stood since 1871. Hans Schmid, the former head of the St Gallen cultural office, revived the palazzo-like, pink-washed building in 2007, transforming it into what it is today: a hotel with 20 very different rooms and a restaurant celebrated for its regional cuisine with an Italian touch. Despite the village's remoteness, there is plenty on offer, including visiting the hotel's own Biblioteca Linard and the regular jazz and classical concerts in the *arvensaal*. A walk around the grounds and in the hills is also recommended on spring days and summer evenings. *ottomesi.ch*

MOUNTAIN HOTEL
BERGHUUS RADONS
Radons, Graubünden

In the village of Radons, this beautifully reimagined wooden lodge stands out. At the heart of Berghuus is Ustereia, a historic restaurant where owner and chef Fadri Arpagaus produces a dining experience grounded in place and memory. He serves mountain dishes enriched with global influences, raises his own specially bred cows and crafts herbal teas from edelweiss and other Alpine flowers. The lodge formerly belonged to a family friend and Arpagaus spent some of his childhood summers here. "I always longed to return and give back to this region," he says. He bought the property in 2019, transforming it with the help of local craftsmen and materials. *berghuus.ch*

MOUNTAIN HOTEL
TSCHUGGEN GRAND
Arosa, Graubünden

In a fairy tale corner of the Swiss Alps, the Tschuggen Grand is easily recognised by its futuristic Mario Botta architecture peeking out from the snowy slopes. Inside, Carlo Rampazzi's classic but playful interiors mix Hermès furniture, cashmere throws and colourful textiles. The 128 rooms and suites are tailored for cocoon-like comfort, with deep armchairs and panoramic mountain views. For après-ski, there is La Brezza (boasting two Michelin stars), while an Alpine-style restaurant, replete with a bowling alley, provides easygoing sport when off the slopes. A private funicular – the Tschuggen Express – spirits guests from the hotel's boot room straight to the ski trails. *tschuggencollection.ch*

MOUNTAIN HOTEL
PONTISELLA
Stampa, Graubünden

"I wanted to awaken a historic building from its slumber," says Daniel Erne of Pontisella in Stampa. He has breathed new life into the 1849 property that was a summer house for the local Pontisella family, who had emigrated to Italy as confectioners. The interior mixes original features with warm, contemporary touches curated by the owner. The four guest rooms include wood panelling, concrete floors and futon-style beds, while communal spaces combine stone fireplaces, pendant lights and mid-century furniture. Guests enjoy a delicious breakfast focusing on organic ingredients sourced from regional producers and farms. *pontisella-stampa.ch*

MOUNTAIN HOTEL
KURHAUS BERGÜN
Bergün, Graubünden

The *kurhaus* – as hotels for reinvigoration were called in this part of *Mitteleuropa* in the early-1900s – has an enduring quality that few buildings of this scale possess and this hotel leans heavily into these now-rare period aspects. Cake is served on mismatched antique dishes, while rooms are sparingly decorated with an emphasis on architectural details, including period wash basins and chandeliers, and art nouveau fittings. "Historical substance can be really valuable," says manager Christof Steiner. Guests can choose to ski, skate, sledge and snow shoe in the Albula Valley and at the end of the day, they can head to the hotel's hot and cold outdoor pools. *kurhausberguen.ch*

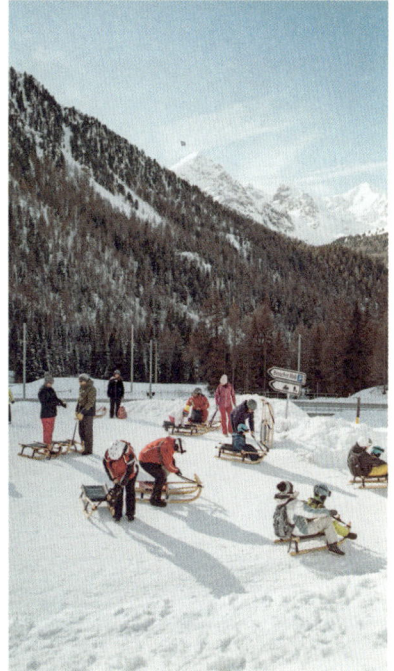

DISCOVER SWITZERLAND | MOUNTAIN HOTELS

CASA CAMINADA
Fürstenau, Graubünden

Fürstenau is one of those idyllic Swiss towns where life moves at a deliberate pace. It's also where chef Andreas Caminada opened his first restaurant in 2003. His three-Michelin-star establishment at Schloss Schauenstein (*pictured, bottom right, behind Caminada*) is the crown jewel of the region's gastronomic map so having a guesthouse on the site quickly became part of the plan. He asked Bündner architect Gion A Caminada (a distant relative) to transform two stables into a contemporary stay. The result is Casa Caminada's 10 tasteful rooms, with a view of Fürstenau and the surrounding mountains.
casacaminada.com

All you need is loaves
Casa Caminada's bakery-cum-épicerie is the heartbeat of the property. Inside, bakers pull one loaf after another out of a wood-fired oven, filling the space with the comforting smell of freshly baked bread. "We want to celebrate craftsmanship," says Caminada. "It brings villagers to us and has helped to rejuvenate the town."

MOUNTAIN HOTEL
BRÜCKE 49
Vals, Graubünden

At the gateway to the Tomül Pass, in the village of Vals, Brücke 49 consists of two remarkable heritage buildings enhanced with Ruth Kramer's artistic flair (*see page 196*). The interior designer has applied her appreciation of natural materials throughout the space, with the stone and wood façade emulated by the furnishings inside. The rooms with inviting fireplaces and views of the town square are an update of a traditional bed and breakfast, while the apartments with kitchens and dining rooms are for guests who wish to stay longer. Stunning scenery and thoughtful design touches, coupled with a great morning spread and a warm ambience, make for a memorable stay. *brucke49.ch*

MOUNTAIN HOTEL
CHESA GRISCHUNA
Klosters, Graubünden

Up in the mountains of Klosters, Hans Guler opened the Chesa Grischuna in 1938. Constructed around an old inn, the building was transformed by architect Hermann Schneider into the spirited hotel it is today. In spite of further refurbishments, original elements of 1930s craftsmanship have been keenly preserved. The rooms feature paintings by acclaimed illustrator Alois Carigiet and local pine in the traditional Graubünden style. The restaurant serves hearty dishes on tableware designed for the space. Owing to its beauty, Chesa Grischuna has hosted many international stars over the years, earning the nickname "Hollywood on the rocks". *chesagrischuna.ch*

MOUNTAIN HOTEL
SUVRETTA HOUSE
St Moritz

In 1911 hotelier Anton Bon stood at the foot of the Upper
Engadine mountains and decided to build a hotel. Today the
storybook castle boasts 171 lavish rooms and 10 suites, and is a
bastion of opulent Alpine luxury. The main lobby opens into
a vast columned space with large windows looking onto
Lake Champfèr. The Grand Restaurant offers French fare by
executive chef Fabrizio Zanetti – a St Moritz local – and
requires formal dress. "People ask me if the tie rule will be
around for long," says co-general manager Peter Egli. "We
say, as long as Hermès does ties, we will keep the tradition."
suvrettahouse.ch

Holiday on ice
In winter Suvretta is transformed into
a wonderland with an ice rink and
ice-sculpture playground for children.
Skiers can rent equipment and the
hotel's own private ski lift shuttles
guests up the mountain.

MOUNTAIN HOTEL
HUUS LÖWEN
Gonten, Appenzell Innerrhoden

Heemelige is how the Huus Löwen team thinks of its hotel in the heart of Gonten, a picturesque village (*pictured*) in the canton of Appenzell Innerrhoden. The word is the local equivalent of Danish *hygge*, a quality of contentment found in all of the 24 rooms. Each features carved wood panels, natural tones and Alpine views typical of the Appenzell region. Chef Carsten Kypke serves the best local produce: the goat's cheese is from the village dairy, the chicken is delivered from the Alpstein region and the angus beef was raised on nearby pastures. In his restaurant, Löwenstobe, try the cheese *spaetzle* with fried onions, apple sauce and boiled sausage after a long hike.
appenzellerhuus.ch

MOUNTAIN HOTEL
ALPENGOLD HOTEL
Davos

Reportedly the choice of world leaders during the World Economic Forum annual meeting, the Alpengold is set between the mountains of the Davos valley. It offers expansive views and respite throughout the year, as well as two bars and five restaurants, including a rooftop outpost of Peruvian-Japanese La Muña. During ski season, a shuttle takes guests directly to some of the best skiing spots in Graubünden on the Alpine slopes and Nordic trails of the Davos-Klosters mountains, while in summer the Alpengold is within walking distance to watersports and swimming on Lake Davos, with easy access to hiking trails.
alpengoldhotel.com

MOUNTAIN HOTEL
YETI HUTS
Grindelwald, Berne

This former shepherd's hut is framed by maple trees and situated on a mountain pasture with a magnificent view of the Grindelwald valley. A flock of sheep graze next to the hut in summer, while in winter sledges and snowshoes are available for tours that start at the house. The Ischboden Alpine Hut is rustic and private with traditional furnishings, its own spring-fed well, a hot outdoor shower and a fireplace for relaxed evenings. In the snow, guests can only reach the retreat by foot or sledge but upon arrival a Grindelwald fondue and fresh bread from the village bakery awaits. *yeti.ch*

The incomparable snowman
This is one of seven idyllic, fully equipped huts in the Jungfrau region of the Bernese Oberland that are run and rented out by local ex-pilot, mountain guide and film-set talent Beat Hutmacher, known as Yeti (*pictured, with his dog Bepito*). "My grandfather lived in Ischboden when he was herding his animals," says Hutmacher, who grew up in the region and knows it like the back of his hand.

MOUNTAIN HOTEL
THE BRECON
Adelboden, Berne

Surrounded by firs and snow-frosted massifs in the Alpine village of Adelboden, The Brecon is a 22-key chalet-turned-guesthouse with a down-to-earth approach to hospitality. Built in 1914, it matches the charms of a Swiss timber cottage with a pared-back palette designed by Amsterdam-based studio Nicemakers. "We want our guests to feel like they are staying at a generous friend's home," says co-owner Grant Maunder. Featuring stone floors, textured woollen upholstery and leather trims, the hotel also hosts a spa and has a stunning outdoor pool nearby (*pictured*). Summers are for hiking and winters are spent skiing in one of three areas nearby.
thebrecon.com

MOUNTAIN HOTEL
GRAND HOTEL BELVEDERE
Wengen, Berne

The secluded village of Wengen is the jewel of the Lauterbrunnen Valley and home of the Grand Hotel Belvedere. Combining tradition with sophisticated modernity, the hotel reopened in May 2025 after renovations that focused on bringing it back to its original belle époque state. "It was essential for us to adopt the Alpine construction philosophy of this era," says Swiss architect Arnaud Christin, who spearheaded the refurbishment. There are two restaurants and two bars, each with distinct atmospheres, while the 90 state-of-the-art rooms and suites are adorned with handmade carpets and bespoke pine furniture.
beaumier.com

MOUNTAIN HOTEL
HOTEL GRIMSEL HOSPIZ
Guttannen, Berne

The historic Hotel Grimsel Hospiz sits at the head of the Grimsel Pass high in the Bernese Alps. Surrounded by towering peaks, the hotel overlooks the turquoise waters of the Oberhasli Reservoir (Lake Grimsel). The castle-like stone building with red shutters was built in 1934, though a hotel has existed on the site since 1142. In summer it is reached via a winding road or by bus. In winter the last stage of the trip is only possible with guidance by hotel staff through a special tunnel and a cable car. A 2010 renovation introduced contemporary elements to the original charm, with warm wool upholstery and furnishings from Swiss manufacturer Horgenglarus.
grimselwelt.ch

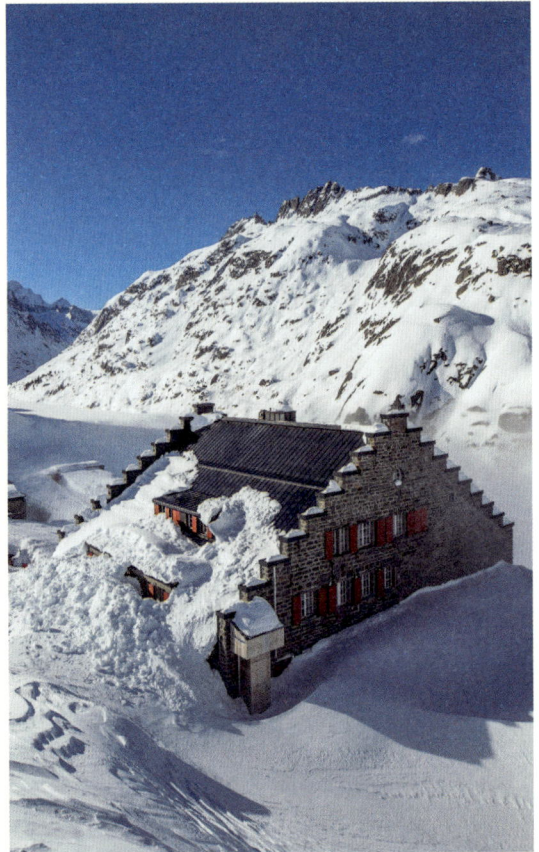

MOUNTAIN HOTEL
CHÂTEAU DE RAYMONTPIERRE
Val Terbi, Jura

This château nestles among the verdant Jura mountains, an area more used to farmers than retreat-goers. Despite extensive renovation, the 16th-century building retains its charm. Guests are served locally sourced food with regional wine pairings, while the spa area and yoga studio's floor-to-ceiling windows provide views of forests and distant mountains. In addition to the main building's six bedrooms, an annexe provides an extra eight. The rooms are unadorned, without televisions or minibars. "We want guests to be immersed in nature and not too distracted," says Sydney Karolewski, who manages the property with partner Timon Wolf.
chateauderaymontpierre.ch

URBAN HOTEL
VILLA CASTAGNOLA
Lugano

In 1880 the Villa Castagnola was built on Lake Lugano to be the residence of the Russian Von Ritter family. Later, a family from Lucerne bought the mansion and turned it into a guesthouse, then an impressive hotel. Since then, it has been a sanctuary for aristocrats, artists and intellectuals, many of who left their mark by adding pieces to the owners' art collection, which is on display in the establishment. Castagnola's 71 rooms and suites all offer a view of the lake and the park below. In the warmer months a private lido lures guests to the water's edge, while chef Alessandro Boleso of the hotel's three restaurants whips up local delicacies.
villacastagnola.com

URBAN HOTEL
BAUR AU LAC
Zürich

Putting down roots
In the hotel's private park is a ginkgo biloba tree that is said to be more than 100 years old. It is claimed that the seed for the tree was a gift from the garden of a visiting Japanese emperor and was planted in 1880. Today it is a point of pride for the hotel and a symbol of its history.

Sitting in a verdant park with views of Lake Zürich and the Alps, this hotel has been charming guests since 1844. Suites are adorned with bespoke furniture and art deco touches while rooms come with cosy reading lamps and access to the private courtyard. The stay is enhanced by the ample dining experiences on offer. Marguita serves Mediterranean-inspired dishes, while classic brasserie Baur's celebrates European cuisine. Le Hall is the perfect spot for a coffee and, come evening, the head sommelier's wine selection takes centre stage. Baur au Lac really does have it all.
bauraulac.ch

URBAN HOTEL
STORCHEN
Zürich

The Storchen is a bastion of Swiss hospitality and opulence. Though the stately exterior remains protected, the hotel was renovated in 1939, 1999 and again in 2017, with the most recent update including its 64 rooms, the Michelin-starred La Rôtisserie and the ever-lively Barchetta Bar. Among the additions was the Nest rooftop terrace, which opens in warm weather and offers a view of the Alps. It's this location that helps to set the Storchen apart from other five-star hotels in the city: the Signature Suite, for example, has views of both the river and the lake (along with magnificent sunrises). *storchen.ch*

Grand designs
Occupying a prized spot on the river Limmat in central Zürich for more than six centuries, the Storchen's name originates from the building's first written record, which mentioned two storks perched atop the roof. The brand's avian emblem is a symbol of the establishment's grace and prestige.

URBAN HOTEL
THE DOLDER GRAND
Zürich

In the Adlisberg hills outside Zürich, The Dolder Grand offers a convenient combination of urban access and restorative vistas. Opened at the end of the 19th century, it was recognised as a two-Michelin-key hotel in 2024 while celebrating its 125th anniversary. "The hotel is an example of timeless elegance," says its general manager, Markus Granelli. "The hotel's history is balanced with forward-thinking innovations." There are 175 luxurious rooms and suites, and numerous restaurants, plus one of the largest spas in Switzerland. Each detail of the mid-2000s redesign was overseen by Foster + Partners, such as a new ballroom and a grand south-facing entrance.
thedoldergrand.com

URBAN HOTEL
SIGNAU HOUSE
Zürich

It's one of Zürich's smallest hotels but Signau House doesn't feel diminutive. Built in 1912 as a two-storey mansion, it was bought in 2018 by three local families, who renovated it, with Swiss firm Edelaar Mosayebi Inderbitzin in charge of the redesign. Hosts Regula Brucker and Tina Wiemes (*pictured, on right, with Brucker*) are now at the helm. Inside are nine guest rooms, a lounge with an open fire, and a 25-seat cinema – an echo of when a film company owned the premises in the 1960s. The idyllic garden pavilion promises privacy and the homely yet tasteful interior features restored herringbone flooring, antique chairs with fabrics by Fischbacher 1819 and Italian sofas by Hoffmann.
signauhouse.com

URBAN HOTEL
HOTEL BEAU SÉJOUR
Lucerne

The Beau Séjour calls itself "*Le petit grand hotel*": the small big hotel. The 27-room establishment opened in its current incarnation in 2018 in an 1875 building on Lake Lucerne. There are intricate parquet floors, three-metre-high ceilings, high-quality bed linen and 1970s-era tiled bathrooms. The interiors are the creation of Swiss designer Daniel Hunziker, with contemporary art by Nina Staehli. One special touch is the collection of hand-drawn portraits by illustrator Hyo-Song Becker of every staff member over the years. "The feel of the portraits has evolved with the hotel," says the Beau Séjour's director, Ferry Wey. *beausejourlucerne.ch*

URBAN HOTEL
HOTEL KRAFFT
Basel

Perched on the Rhine, Hotel Krafft is a charming outpost steeped in history. Spanning five breathtaking floors, it exhibits a blend of classic and modern influences. Original 19th-century details – including the lobby tiles and staircase railing – sit alongside mid-century furniture in high-ceilinged common areas adorned with delicate stucco work. Guests are encouraged to venture out on the free-of-charge bikes provided. The intimate restaurant serves French cuisine and diners can enjoy a meal on the terrace or inside, with its large windows and original herringbone flooring. For quiet evenings, Salon Bleu is an inviting den where guests can read and have a nightcap. *krafftbasel.ch*

URBAN HOTEL
BELLEVUE PALACE
Berne

With sweeping views of the Bernese Alps, this institution has stories to tell. The stained-glass dome in the hall is the first feature to see, followed by historic chandeliers and neoclassical frescoes. Dubbed the guesthouse of the Swiss Confederation, the hotel neighbours the Swiss Parliament and was purchased by the state in 1976 to prevent a Soviet investor from buying it. British novelist John le Carré was a regular and set scenes in his espionage thrillers here. "Berne is very Calvinist," says the hotel's manager, Urs Bührer, referring to the Swiss tendency to keep a low profile. "We are not Monte Carlo. But this is where politicians, diplomats, CEOs and bankers meet."
bellevue-palace.ch

URBAN HOTEL
AUBERGE DU MOUTON
Porrentruy, Jura

Room to roam
The sequestered, forest-lined Jura canton that Auberge du Mouton calls home is a vital part of its image. "There's an authenticity to Porrentruy that is hard to find elsewhere," says co-owner Rebecca Leaver. "We want the hotel to appeal to a youthful, design-conscious clientele looking to explore a largely undiscovered area."

Auberge du Mouton, a 12-key hotel in Porrentruy, Jura, demonstrates a mastery of stripped-back luxury. The 18th-century former school has exposed white brick walls, herringbone floors and lofty wooden beams. It's a simple aesthetic that its owners, Rebecca Leaver and her partner, Samuel Tobler, executed by enlisting the help of Zürich-based interior designers Studio Ottawa in 2023. The resulting project combines the rustic elements of Swiss heritage architecture with light, modern touches. Don't miss the restaurant, which serves seasonal market-based dishes with Swiss organic wines. *dumouton.ch*

URBAN HOTEL
THE WOODWARD
Geneva

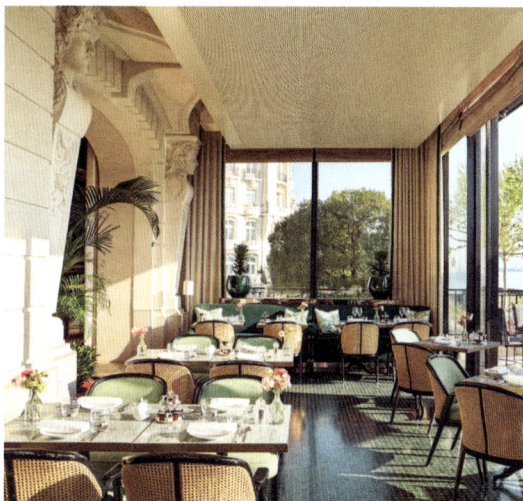

The views from this 26-suite hotel on Lake Geneva take in Mont Blanc and the glittering water of the Bains des Pâquis pool. Its interior design by architect Pierre-Yves Rochon is opulent without heaviness. Think sumptuous linens, silk wallpapers and sunny balconies: every corner is comfortable and welcoming but still refined. "To serve our guests means to care for them," says the executive chef, Olivier Jean (*pictured*), who runs the two Michelin-starred restaurants: L'Atelier Robuchon and Le Jardinier. The spa features a 21-metre indoor swimming pool, saunas and steam rooms that make for a relaxing, rejuvenating stay.
aubergeresorts.com

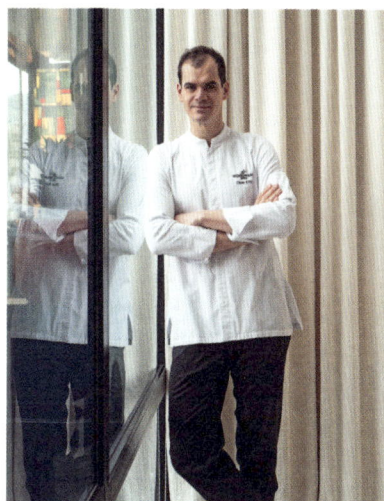

Swiss hosting ranges from stately belle époque palaces to isolated
rural inns and chic modernist hideaways. We talk to four leading
hoteliers about their experiences in the industry.

MEET THE EXPERTS

GÜNTER WEILGUNI
The Home, Zürich

Seasoned hotelier Günter Weilguni opened The Home
hotel in Zürich in 2024 with his brother Manfred.
Weilguni, who specialises in conceptual design and
telling stories, took the Dadaist movement of the early
20th century as inspiration.

How does Dada manifest itself in the interior design?
Unlike many traditional city hotels, which often have
a standard aesthetic, we wanted to create something
that stands out. Every detail was developed with the
intention of conveying the energy of Dadaism. We used
various collage techniques, textures and patterns – not
least on the "Do Not Disturb" signs and room keys.

*The Home is in a former paper factory on the Sihl. What
challenges did you face during the renovation?*
Several. For example, the columns in the hotel were
not allowed to be removed, repainted or covered. The
architects transformed them into tree-like structures
using greenery and lighting.

What should guests expect at the hotel's Loulou restaurant?
At Loulou we serve French cuisine and the signature dish
is the Butcher's Pan Café de Paris. We refer to it as "the
diva of the menu". We have an open kitchen and the
dining room has a great atmosphere.
thehomehotel.ch

HOTELIER
RICHARD LEUENBERGER
Badrutt's Palace, St Moritz

Overlooking the majestic Engadine mountains in St Moritz, 129-year-old Badrutt's Palace is an enduring icon of Alpine elegance. We speak with the hotel's managing director, Richard Leuenberger, who has more than two decades of experience in hospitality and has been at the hotel since 2016.

What excites you about luxury travel?
Hotels have always fascinated me. Travelling extensively as a child, I was captivated by how great hotels create a sense of belonging, even in unfamiliar places. In 2016 my vision for Badrutt's Palace was clear: to honour its rich history and tradition while keeping it relevant to today's ultra-luxury traveller.

What should guests expect from a day at Badrutt's Palace?
For our guests, it would begin in their suite with a butler check-in and an extravagant breakfast experience. Maybe an afternoon tea in Le Grand Hall, St Moritz's secret living room, where many guests spend an entire afternoon enjoying the atmosphere to the sound of the piano. Then there is our mountain restaurant, Paradiso, directly on the ski slope, or our Chesa Veglia, the oldest farmhouse in St Moritz, home to four restaurants in winter. There's also the option of an evening at our Renaissance Bar, where you can enjoy a cigar from the 1960s.

How do you honour the hotel's history while not making it feel dated?
We collaborate with designers such as Champalimaud, who work alongside artisans and our in-house historian to ensure that every detail remains in harmony with the Palace's DNA.
badruttspalace.com

HOTELIERS
JAMES & NATACHA BARON
Krone Säumerei am Inn, Graubünden

James and Natacha Baron run the historic 18-room Krone Säumerei am Inn in Upper Engadine. The pair met in Austria while working at a hotel where James, who is from the UK, was the head chef and Natacha, who is Swiss-Thai, worked in service. The couple lived in Hong Kong and Cambodia before taking over the Krone hotel in 2022 and, within three months, its restaurant, La Chavallera, was awarded a Michelin star.

What was your experience of opening the hotel?
JB: Since it was during the pandemic, we couldn't look at the property before starting to work there, and then we had two and a half weeks to open. You have to learn quickly – it took us a year to feel stable.

Is this region friendly to entrepreneurs?
JB: Absolutely. We weren't expecting such a warm welcome. There isn't the one-upmanship that you see elsewhere. Hoteliers and businesses in the area are a very tight-knit society.
NB: We are quite remote here and the tourism is seasonal, so we need each other. It's just a natural agreement.

What is your favourite thing about the region?
JB: The Engadine is a special place in terms of the light. When the sun goes down everything in the valley turns blue: we call it the blue hour and it's magical.

What are the challenges of working as a couple?
NB: It can be stressful, for sure. You are constantly talking about the hotel and spend a lot of time together but you just need to be aware of that and have your own spaces.
krone-lapunt.ch

Switzerland's culinary landscape is incredibly diverse, taking in both traditional and cutting-edge influences in every field. Here is our selection of the nation's most celebrated gastronomic talents.

DRINKING & DINING

Nowhere else will you find so many restaurants where newspapers on reading sticks, starched napkins and candle-drip catchers with decorative embossing still rule. Old-world charm and attentive service make dining in Switzerland a whimsical experience. This, however, doesn't mean that time-tested establishments are the only option. We scoured the 26 cantons for the best concepts to excite your palate: from lavish dishes served beneath the glint of a giant disco ball to ski-in culinary *cabanes* (huts). Osterias, brasseries and *stübli* are good places to understand the rich blend of cultural influences in Switzerland. You'll soon learn that local gastronomy encompasses much more than chocolate, cheese fondue and Birchermüesli. Swiss viticulture might be one of the lesser-known crafts worth exploring: homegrown wine is so popular with residents that only about 1 per cent is exported. So on your next trip, look out for fendant, petite arvine and cornalin – varieties not easy to find beyond the borders.

THE EDIT

1 **Restaurants**
From cosy mountain inns to hip urban lunch counters, it's all here.

2 **Bars**
Everything from relaxed alfresco wine bars to retro disco dance halls.

3 **Wineries**
Dedicated specialists producing uniquely Swiss bottles.

4 **Cafés**
Ideal spots to sit, relax and get your daily caffeine fix.

5 **Bakeries**
Expert makers of bread and pastries: some traditional, some innovative.

6 **Chocolatiers**
Switzerland's tastiest soft-power industry.

7 **Fromageries**
Fresh mountain grass leads to happy cows and exquisite cheese.

8 **Food retailers and bottle shops**
Flavourful specialists for the finest in Swiss food and wine.

9 **Markets**
The best places to stock up on the freshest provisions.

10 **The experts**
Four insiders tell us how to get ahead.

RESTAURANT

CHOUPETTE
Zürich

This colourful, modern brasserie is five minutes on foot from Lake Zürich and is connected to the Hotel Locke am Platz. "We are not a classic brasserie," says managing director and co-owner Dino Schön. "We focus on a modern, progressive style of cooking with a strong regional focus – seasonal products from trusted local producers, interpreted in a creative way." *Kalbshackbraten* with potato purée, root vegetables and truffle jus is a particular favourite. The tartares are freshly prepared and an excellent wine list with a focus on French wines complements the delicious dishes. *choupette.zuerich*

Dipping culture
Choupette's modern, urban interior design was created by London-based Tatjana von Stein, who also furnished the flats and rooms of Locke Living's aparthotel. When the evenings are milder, 40 outdoor seats are available for a sundowner – perhaps after a swim in the nearby Seebad Enge.

RESTAURANT
OXEN
Küsnacht, Zürich

Once a traditional restaurant going by the name Ochsen, Oxen serves up reimagined dishes of hearty classics while staying true to the spirit of the neighbourhood. Near the Lake Zürich shore, it was founded by MONOCLE and *Konfekt* editorial director and chairman Tyler Brûlé and associates Marc Wegenstein, Markus Binkert and Thomas Maechler. Oxen offers seasonal dishes such as the juicy Oxen burger, braised baby lettuce with chilli gremolata, and a white brownie with macadamia nuts. There are also seven sleeper car-inspired guestrooms and a Monocle Apartment for overnight stays. *oxen.ch*

Room with a moo
For those wishing to extend the experience, Oxen offers seven comfortable rooms in the spirit of the traditional *gasthof* (inn), decorated in a minimalist, mid-modern Swiss style. A Monocle Apartment complete with two bedrooms can be found on the second floor of the space, ideal for a relaxing long-weekend getaway.

RESTAURANT
GÜL
Zürich

Chef Elif Oskan got her start in cuisine naturally – it was deeply rooted in her Turkish childhood. "Anyone of Turkish heritage would say that food, more than anything, is about community, about gathering," she says. Together with her partner, Markus Stöckle, Oskan owns Gül, where seasonal Turkish cooking meets open-fire tradition and is always served to share. When launching this restaurant, Oskan sought to make it a place of comfort and conversation, drawing from memories of meals cooked by her mother. "It's deeply emotional for me to be able to share all this with guests, and it's very much a collective effort," says Oskan. *guel.ch*

RESTAURANT
SCHNUPF
Zürich

On a quiet corner in Zürich's up-and-coming Aussersihl neighbourhood, this restaurant-cum-bar serves quality dishes and drinks in its low-lit dining room and in a shaded garden on sunny days. Co-managed by Vanda Cham Kunz and Rodrigo Zimmermann, this welcoming venue strikes the perfect balance between sophistication and informality. "No pretense, no gimmicks – honest and human gastronomy," says Zimmermann. House favourites are artichokes served with a delicate vinaigrette, sardines in extra-virgin olive oil with parsley salad and toast, and a perfectly seared steak sourced from Ojo de Agua. *schnupf.bar*

RESTAURANT
SAMIGO AMUSEMENT
Zürich

RESTAURANT
HOI KOI
Zürich

Hoi Koi's ever-changing seasonal menu is the creation of chef Zhou Qinhan (*pictured*), who prepares dishes with creativity and flair. Qinhan offers *shabu shabu* (Japanese hot pot) in the colder months, plenty of vegan options and bento boxes for lunch. The interior was designed by Swiss studio Pfeffermint, and they combined marble counter space with birch plywood to add a lighter quality to the dark red walls and table tops. Hoi Koi also offers a selection of sake, Japanese whiskies and plum wine. In addition to the usual Japanese plates, we recommend the natto with quail egg – an authentic dish of traditionally fermented soybeans with rice.
hoikoi.ch

Samigo Amusement offers gastronomy and outdoor sports in a unique and colourful way. Overlooking Lake Zürich, the restaurant is on the ground floor and in the garden while the roof has a sports area offering boxing, yoga, basketball and bootcamps. The menu fuels diners with flavourful choices, including zander tempura, chicken waffles, the ever-classic cheeseburger, and mortadella pizza with *stracciatella di burrata*, pistachios and lemon. Plus, there's Sunday brunch and selections of iced treats for summer days. On Saturday nights the rooftop court is transformed into an open-air club, with a DJ and signature cocktails.
samigo.ch

RESTAURANT
OSSO
Zürich

This buzzy restaurant in Zürich's popular late-night neighbourhood of Langstrasse is where to go for hearty, filling plates. Osso offers breakfast, lunch and dinner on weekdays and is also open for dinner on Saturdays. The atmosphere is further elevated by refined menus that highlight sharing plates made from regional produce and a well-chosen wine list. Bread is baked in-house and the relaxed interior design features floor-to-ceiling windows allowing a view across Langstrasse, making for a truly social Swiss experience.
ossozuerich.ch

Credit: Swiss
Osso touts the highlights of Swiss cuisine while also embracing new and exciting dishes. The restaurant takes an environmentally conscious approach, with many of its ingredients locally sourced and cooked to order on the kitchen's open grill.

RESTAURANT
KRONENHALLE
Zürich

Picture perfect
Kronenhalle's rules are strict: no video calls, minimal screens and no athleisurewear, please. Removed from their phones, guests can soak in their surroundings. Paintings by European greats including Chagall, Miró and Picasso (many of who were guests) adorn the walls, accompanied by a portrait of Hulda Zumsteg, who co-founded the restaurant in 1924.

In its central location near Zürich's Opera House and Quai Bridge, Kronenhalle is one of the city's most venerable institutions. Famed for its impeccable service and delectable takes on French and Swiss classics, the restaurant has perfected the art of understated hospitality. Lights are dimmed, chandeliers sparkle and uniformed waiting staff sail between tables like Swiss clockwork. Today the head chef is Peter Schärer, who has been part of the kitchen staff for more than 30 years. So take a seat and order some veal with *rösti* and a crisp glass of sauvignon blanc. This is old-world Zürich at its best.
kronenhalle.com

RESTAURANT
REBSTOCK
Baden

Rebstock's terrace is one of Baden's best in the summer, with trees and flowering vines, but it's the food that really draws guests. Swiss-Tamil chef Ahilan Jayaverasinhe has led the Rebstock kitchen since it opened. His menu offers main courses including spiced autumn game platters and cordon bleu. Jayaverasinhe also turns out a delicious lamb curry and the fiery Pasta Ahilan, which has a legion of fans. "The most beautiful thing is when people start talking to the table next to them, maybe order a bottle of wine and stay to enjoy it," says Myriam Meyer (*pictured*), one of Rebstock's three owners. *rebstockbaden.ch*

Social drinking
At Rebstock, carafes of water are filled from its central fountain – guests are invited to retrieve their own refills of cold, free-flowing Swiss drinking water.

RESTAURANT
CASA NOVO
Berne

When Casa Novo's founders Dominik and Jesús Novo stepped down from their restaurant in 2023 after almost 20 years, they knew it was in safe hands. New owner Dirk Wagner, Casa Novo's long-time head chef, has since steered the Mediterranean menu gently towards the international crowd while homing in on regional produce. Depending on the season there might be Swiss veal with polenta and mushrooms, cauliflower steak with cranberries and chickpeas or the house classic: beef tenderloin tartare. There are menus of three to six courses too, with tapas served from 17.00 to 19.00. casa-novo.ch

Alfresco shining
The Casa Novo terrace is one of the prettiest in the old town, overlooking the jumble of medieval riverside townhouses and suspended above the Aare river. Whether bathed in light during the day or wrapped in a twinkling glow in the evening, Wagner's philosophy is that "going out" should feel like coming home.

RESTAURANT
VOLKSHAUS
Basel

Designed by Basel-based architecture firm Herzog & de Meuron, the Volkshaus is peppered with green leather that blends nicely with the verdant courtyard. Evenings begin at the bar, sipping signature negronis and sitting amid art from the owners' collection. From there, it's into the brasserie where neighbours, families and corporate colleagues enjoy *cuisine du marché*, served by a friendly, dedicated staff. "The challenge for me personally is to find the right staff with the combined personality traits of openness and authenticity," says Volkshaus general manager Manuela Voser.
volkshaus-basel.ch

Rhine and spirit
The Kleinbasel neighbourhood lies on the eclectic side of the Rhine, across from the cathedral and the old city. Here, the Volkshaus caters to the community and to guests visiting the likes of Art Basel (*see pages 138 and 146*) or attending meetings at the pharmaceutical hubs. "The mixture of guests is what makes the brasserie," says Voser.

BRASSERIE BODU
Lucerne

A self-proclaimed *Französische* brasserie, or French brasserie, Bodu feels more like an art deco Parisian outpost than a Swiss *stübli*. It's a panacea for homesick French expats living in this German-speaking canton. In the past two decades, Bodu has provided familiar fare for its Francophile clientele and amassed a loyal following. Classics such as salad niçoise, bouillabaisse and moules-frites are all here in their Gallic splendour. But this wouldn't be a brasserie without a well-researched wine list: that's why each year the Bodu team makes a pilgrimage to the vineyards of Bordeaux to scope out the finest wine from new châteaux to house in Bodu's cellar. *brasseriebodu.ch*

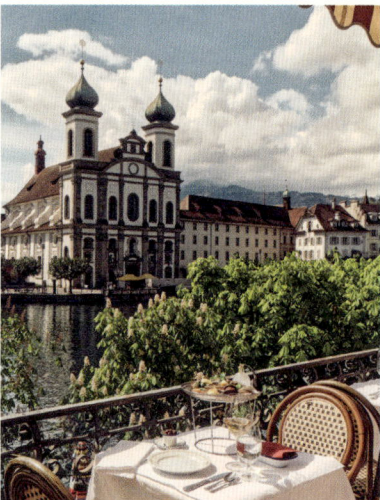

BLEU NUIT
Geneva

When Florian Le Bouhec took over Bleu Nuit with Mathias Fréré – his former colleague at bistronomic restaurant Le Bologne – he wanted to add to Geneva's vibrant culinary scene. At Bleu Nuit, diners perch at the long steel bar for a plate of charcuterie or a fine selection of cheeses from local cheesemaker Bruand. "I like to shake up the established Swiss gastronomic codes and come up with creative compositions," says Le Bouhec of his menu, which changes weekly. To those in the know, more is to be found behind closed doors. Through a refrigerator-cum-portal door at the back of the restaurant, guests are invited to Le Frigo, Bleu Nuit's speakeasy. *Rue du Vieux-Billard 4, 1205*

RESTAURANT
BOMBAR
Geneva

Bombar – designed to sound like bon bar, meaning good bar – is deliberately minimalistic yet meticulously planned out. "I take food and wine seriously but I'm unfussy about it," says owner Marc Popper, who purchased the space in 2019. The low-intervention wine list includes European heavyweights such as those from the Jura, Beaujolais and Savoie regions, alongside local wines. "We want to target a curious, fun-loving clientele," says Popper. Indeed, there's something festive about Bombar's relaxed approach to mealtimes. Dinner is served until 22.30, which is practically unheard of in Geneva. We'll drink to that. *bombar.ch*

Called to the bar
Everything from the starched napkins to the dim lighting and wooden furniture has been carefully considered at Bombar: especially the stainless-steel counter. "I love sitting at the bar when I'm in a new city because you're in on the action," says Popper. "People don't expect to eat well when sitting at a counter and that's a perception we want to change."

RESTAURANT
ROBERTO
Geneva

The generations of Genevans who choose to return to Roberto, established in 1945, is testament to the restaurant's unwavering dedication to genuine Italian fare. Roberto Carugati wanted to create an Italian-style trattoria emblematic of the flavours of his homeland. A proud member of the Accademia Italiana della Cucina that protects Italy's culinary heritage all around the world, the Carugati family is devoted to the efforts of their forefathers. We recommend the silky tomato and basil risotto, which uses Tuscan olive oil and Carnaroli rice, finished with fresh butter and parmigiano reggiano.
restaurantroberto.ch

Old-country fare
Today, Carugati's grandson Alexandre Campa (*pictured*) heads the kitchen using ingredients of superlative quality, including tomatoes sourced from Pachino: "The favourable microclimate allows the tomatoes to grow year-round," says Campa, who gets his white truffles from Alba and *guanciale* from Umbria.

RESTAURANT
CAFÉ DE LA PAIX
Geneva

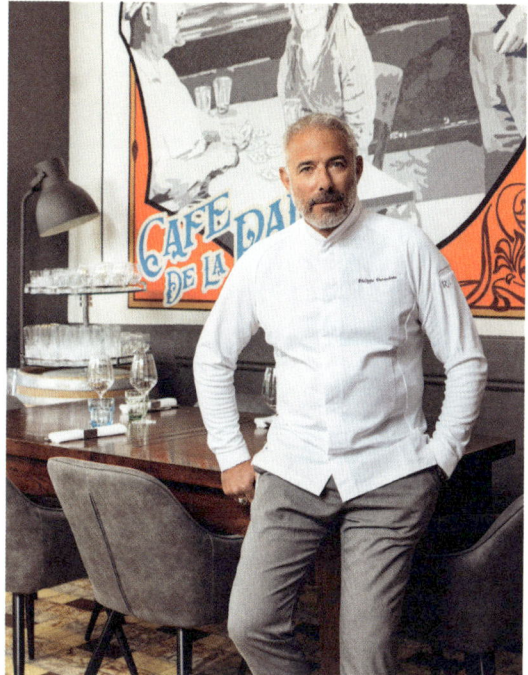

Café de la Paix is one of Geneva's oldest bistros and a charming space where fêted chef Philippe Durandeau (*pictured*) serves meals that celebrate the subject of each dish. Favourites include beef *tagliata* with parmesan and rocket, while the café's signature calamaretti is testament to Durandeau's taste. The menu is enhanced by the restaurant's design: outside, the leafy terrace hosts diners on summer evenings while the interior is an homage to 1960s Parisian design. Classic wooden furniture and vintage tiles are complemented by art deco chandeliers and wine-lined walls of carefully chosen bottles.

cafe-delapaix.ch

RESTAURANT
CABANE MONT FORT
Verbier

Poised at 2,457 metres, this restaurant's remoteness makes it exclusive but no less welcoming. With stunning panoramas of Mont Blanc and the Grand Combin massifs, the cottage was built in 1925 as a mountaineers' shelter but has become a culinary destination. The journey is rewarded with grilled veal sausages and cheesy croûtes, Valais vintages and La Nébuleuse beer. Cabane Mont Fort is also a 15-key mountain refuge where ski-in ski-out has never been more literal. "Being accessible only on skis and on foot during the winter means we welcome an informed clientele aware of the challenges of high-altitude environments," says co-manager Audrey Galas.
cabanemontfort.com

RESTAURANT
CHEZ DANY
Verbier

Verbier is by no means devoid of glitzy mountaintop restaurants but Chez Dany sets itself apart. The high-altitude hangout offers elevated Swiss fare, including croûtes with local bagnes cheese and topped with a fried egg, smoked trout with sauce vierge, and an oozy baked camembert with pear jam. But the seasonal menu's influences cross borders, proffering a Helvetic spin on Iberian croquetas and Milanese ossobuco. Evenings at Chez Dany feature venison and rump steak while the fondue machine is fired up for decadent Valaisan feasts. Diners can then hop on the establishment's snowcat to get back to Verbier if the toboggan isn't your thing.
chezdany.ch

RESTAURANT
ALTER TORKEL
Jenins, Graubünden

A fine vintage
The self-proclaimed "Huus vum Bündner Wii" (House of Grisons Wine) has its roots in a 17th-century village wine press and the community aspect is still central at Alter Torkel: a 2015 addition contains an exhibition room for the Graubünden Wein industry association. More than 1,500 bottles are available in the restaurant's *weinarchiv*, demonstrating the depth and range of the small region.

Each spring, when the last Graubünden snows melt, the Alter Torkel terrace is perhaps at its freshest. The simple stone building holds a commanding position over the Bündner Herrschaft wine region, situated in the middle of lush grapevines and surrounded by snowcapped mountains. The microclimate is perfect for pinot noir, riesling silvaner and other regional varietals. The restaurant was taken over in 2020 by Julia and Oliver Friedrich and the latter regularly chooses a selection of mostly local wines before the kitchen team, headed by chef David Esser, matches them with seasonal, regional (and sometimes international) dishes.
alter-torkel.ch

RESTAURANT
RÖSSLI
Feutersoey-Gstaad, Berne

In 2019, a century after its opening, Sabine Köll and Simon Richard (*pictured*) took over Rössli. Köll, head of service at the restaurant, and Richard, head of cuisine, both earned their spurs during three years at the Michelin-starred Chesa Pirani in La Punt on the team of chef Daniel Bumann. "We felt the time was right for our own business," says Köll. The Rössli classics that have contributed to the restaurant's status include the regional blue trout and the Viennese schnitzel made with Simmental veal. In winter, the wood-panelled dining room offers up to 40 seats, which in summer expands to a terrace beneath the trees in the garden. *restaurantroessli.swiss*

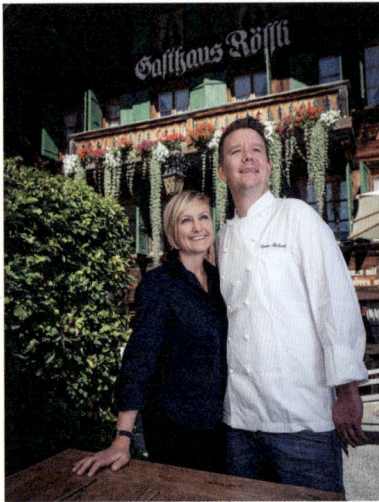

RESTAURANT
LANGOSTERIA
St Moritz

On snow-capped Corviglia above St Moritz is a fine-dining experience that justifies the ski lift journey to 2,000 metres above sea level. With a partially open kitchen behind glass tanks filled with live Alaskan king crabs, Spanish langoustines and Sicilian red prawns, Langosteria promises a culinary experience unlike any other. The main dishes are simple but sumptuous: baked Huelva royal langoustines with Amalfi lemon and aromatic herbs, shell-fresh clams tossed with tomatoes, and linguine with blue lobster. The complex theatrics are saved for dessert: be prepared for the tiramisu, a multilayered customer favourite. *langosteria.com*

RESTAURANT
KULM COUNTRY CLUB
St Moritz

Placed in the expert hands of culinary maestro Mauro Colagreco, the menu at Kulm Country Club in the grounds of the Kulm Hotel (*pictured, top and bottom right*) showcases local produce with a mixture of international dishes and Engadine specialities. At the top of the menu is tagliolini with mountain herb pesto, parmigiano reggiano and toasted pine nuts, yet the restaurant is perhaps best known for its fiery dishes, with many plates containing grilled, smoked and roasted elements. There's a welcoming combination of vintage sledges lining the ceiling and warm wooden furniture, while diners can enjoy an ambient soundtrack and mountain views. *kulm.com*

RESTAURANT BERGFÜHRER
Sertig Dörfli, Graubünden

In the Sertig valley – which blushes a verdant green
in summer and is blanketed by snow in winter – is the
Restaurant Bergführer, a 450-year-old establishment now
the domain of chef Nina Eyer (*pictured*). "The Bergführer
is *einzigartig*, which means unique," she says. "It's special,
thanks to the food and service." The veal cheeks in red
wine sauce, mushroom ravioli with cranberries and beef
tartare are all perfectly seasoned and Eyer is known to
add a pop of spice balanced by deep umami and bright
citrus. The dining room offers expansive views of the
16th-century manor homes and mountains. In Swiss style,
patrons arrive by skis, hiking boots and even horseback.
sertigtal.ch

RESTAURANT
BRASSERIE KONRAD
Engelberg, Obwalden

Brasserie Konrad at Ski Lodge Engelberg serves the best of Swiss comfort food after a long day on the slopes. The menu is shaped by chef Oscar Larsson's international experience, blending European cooking techniques with respect for local ingredients. Dishes such as saltbaked celeriac, vinegar-glazed mangalitza collar with yellow pea purée and black angus and onion tartare mirror the seasons and keep customers coming back. "In a village such as Engelberg, fresh ingredients are a big focus for us," Larsson says, adding that seasonal produce is at the heart of many dishes. *skilodgeengelberg.com*

Village elder
Brasserie Konrad is named after the founder of Engelberg, Konrad von Sellenbüren, and is inspired by the informal and lively atmosphere of a classic brasserie.

BAR
KUNSTHAUS BAR
Zürich

Kunsthaus Bar is a place for encounters between art and cuisine. "The mix of culture and gastronomic experience makes the place unique and important for Zürich," says owner Mischa Dieterich, who brought in seasoned host Ioannis Siamanis (*pictured*) as general manager. Designed by David Chipperfield Architects as a companion for the neighbouring museums, the space features a marble bar with emerald green stools and plush red booths beneath sweeping light fixtures. But the highlight is the original 1934 surrealist painting by artist Max Ernst titled "Pétales et Jardin de la Nymphe Ancolie" that the interior matches in colour palette and style.
kunsthausbar.ch

BAR
CHARLATAN RESTODISCO
Zürich

Charlatan Restodisco is a rare establishment where haute cuisine meets the dance floor (featuring one of the largest disco balls in Europe). Established in 2022, the venue offers a mix of lavish dishes such as lobster pasta and oysters, with drinks including the punchy Charlatan Tiki (rum, pineapple, amaretto and Cointreau). It is open from 18.00 on Wednesdays to Saturdays and the disco starts at 22.00. "We want our guests to feel glamorous, like they've stepped into a different world for the night," says co-owner Patrick Calame-Longjean (*pictured*). "It's a mix of elegance, extravagance and effortless fun."
restodisco.ch

BAR
CONSUM
Basel

In 2002, the new operators of the Krafft Hotel (*see page 38*) had a conundrum: their building had no bar. Across the street stood a bricked-up grocery store. "They looked at it and said, 'This is a hidden gem'," says Jonas Gass, COO of Krafft Gruppe. They turned it into Consum, a Barcelona-inspired wine bar that serves as the hotel's de facto canteen and a hub for Rhine swimmers, passers-by and anyone who wants a good glass of wine. "Always packed full, uncomplicated," is how Gass describes Consum. On warm days people spill into the neighbourhood, while the tables on both sides of the narrow street turn evenings into impromptu block parties.
consumbasel.ch

BAR
MARIUS
Geneva

This bar sits in a century-old *boucherie* (butchers) converted in the early 2000s. When Marc Popper took over Marius in 2023, he envisioned something between a Basque *pintxo* bar and a Japanese *izakaya*, featuring an evolving, imaginative menu of sharing dishes cooked on a Japanese grill. He preserved most of its interior: mixed diamond tiles and a marble counter, which create a simple, unpretentious finish hard to come by in a rapidly developing area. Hearty plates have included Spanish *gildas* (anchovy, guindilla pepper and a green olive on a mini skewer), smokey mushrooms with an egg yolk and endives tossed in a miso vinaigrette.
9 place des Augustins, 1205

WINERY
DOMAINE BLATTNER
Soyhières, Jura

In the northwestern canton of Jura is Domaine Blattner, a winery founded in 1991 by Silvia and Valentin Blattner. The winery is renowned for breeding fungi-resistant grapes, reducing pesticide use and limiting mechanical intervention. Thanks to these meticulous practices, visitors can enjoy organic red and white wines alongside regional delicacies. "By blending innovative grape varieties with a deep respect for tradition, we strive to craft wines that tell the story of our family estate," says Olivia Hänggi-Blattner (*pictured*), who now runs the estate, offering tastings, vineyard tours, cellar visits and other events throughout the year.
domaineblattner.ch

WINERY
ST JODERN KELLEREI
Visperterminen, Valais

The St Jodern Kellerei in Visperterminen is not only the guardian of one of the highest vineyards in Europe, but is also the address of the famous wines vinified with the heida grape (also known as savagnin). The winery is 900 metres above sea level and the St Jodern estate dates from 1979, a time when autochthonous varieties such as heida were unpopular in the Valais region. Today the grape is a highlight, seducing the palate with notes of papaya, honey, roses and ginger. It is delicate yet potent, with a crunchy acidity. It can be sampled at the renovated winery that is built into the mountain, not far from the high-altitude vines that supply it.
jodernkellerei.ch

OBRECHT WEINGUT
Jenins, Graubünden

Wine weather
The winery is in a helpful microclimate: pinot noir particularly thrives in its mild autumnal weather and calcareous soils. The terroir is evident in the winery's output and Obrecht Weingut's top wine, Monolith, has a unique fullness, power and lively finish. The crisp brut rosé is another popular choice and is made from pinot noir and pinot meunier grapes.

Winemakers Francisca (*pictured, right*) and Christian Obrecht (*pictured, above*) met during their studies and today run one of the most visionary wineries in the Bündner Herrschaft. The duo have a holistic way of keeping their grapevines strong. "We promote soil health and the immune system of the plants," says Christian, who has wanted to run the family vineyard since childhood. Changes have occurred under their direction, such as the introduction of a self-service wine-o-mat that offers refrigerated bottles to visitors looking for a chilled glass of something to sip in the sunkissed vineyards. *obrecht.ch*

CAFÉ
LA STANZA
Zürich

Schoolfriends and restaurateurs Livio Notaro, Michele Bernasconi, Jonas Herde and Daniel Ferrari run five Zürich hospitality projects but La Stanza is the original. The ambient coffee bar wouldn't feel out of place in Milan, though the art nouveau interior invites a sense of Manhattan historical charm, complete with high ceilings and a bar crafted by a woodworker from Bergamo. "When we opened in 2008, there was no real Italian coffee in Zürich," says Notaro. From dawn until dusk, politicians and financiers frequent La Stanza for its coffee, its choice of print newspapers and the chilled jazz playlists curated in-house.
lastanza.ch

CAFÉ
NUDE
Zürich

On the bank of the river Limmat, Nude stands out with its yellow tables, floor-to-ceiling A-frame windows and steady hum of chatter. Although normally bustling and in the centre of the Wipkingen quarter of the city, the café has an uncrowded quality thanks to its spaciousness, both inside and out. The award-winning concrete building was designed by Estudio Barozzi Veiga and shares the riverside space with Tanzhaus Zürich, a contemporary dance studio. Although the Tanzhaus takes a summer hiatus, the café is open daily all year round, making it a reliable location for good coffee and a catch-up with friends.
nude-zurich.com

CAFÉ
MIRÓ
Zürich

Brothers David and Daniel Sanchez (*pictured, left to right*) brewed their idea for a boutique café and roastery with little more than a Probat roaster in an empty garage. Their flagship store in central Zürich has concrete walls, metal shelving and a minimalist bar, which are softened by lush foliage, floor-to-ceiling windows and the enticing aromas of pastries and freshly roasted beans. From Mexican El Sueño decaf and Colombian Los Nogales to Ethiopian Harbegona and Kenyan Massai beans, Miró produces delicious speciality coffee. Stop by the brothers' coffee truck, which can be spotted on the streets of Zürich, for the perfect pick-me-up on the go.
mirocoffee.co

CAFÉ
MONOCLE CAFÉ
Zürich

Since 2018 the Monocle Café has been a staple establishment and – we like to think – a top address to grab a coffee. A short walk from Zürichsee, the space was designed by David Marquardt from Mach Architektur (*see page 192*). There is room for patrons to dine, shop, study or catch up with friends and the seats spill onto the pavement, where MONOCLE readers congregate when the Swiss sun obliges. The café serves sandwiches, *flammkuchen* (German flatbread) and Japanese baked goods from nearby bakeries Hiro Takahashi (*see page 85*) and Atelier Okashi. Visitors can also enjoy an aperitif while staff file reports from the bureau overhead.
monocle.com

CAFÉ
MILL'FEUILLE
Lucerne

CAFÉ
BELMONT
St Moritz

Teetering on the banks of the Reuss in medieval Lucerne, Mill'Feuille's terrace is a good place to start the day. Breakfast is served until 11.00 (14.00 at weekends), so you can take your time. "We want to create an uncomplicated, comfortable atmosphere," says co-owner Samuel Vörös, who established Mill'Feuille in 2014. From apple *streuselkuchen* and cheesecake to *tarte aux pommes* and chocolate brownies made in-house, Mill'Feuille even has the coveted Fait Maison accolade. Favourites on the ever-rotating lunchtime menu include smoked salmon on pumpernickel with miso mayo, battered trout and a poached char fillet.
millfeuille.ch

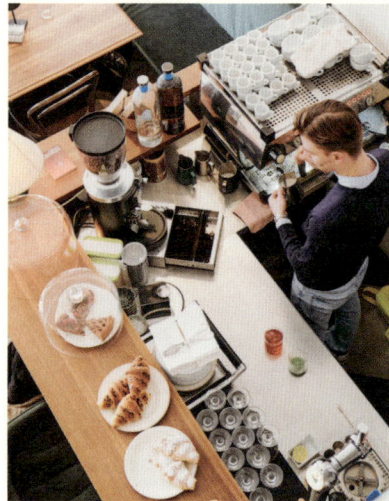

When Silvano Vitalini heard that a well-located bar in his adopted hometown was closing, he decided to take it over. The fashion entrepreneur was a frequent customer and the space became a passion project. "I'm here almost every day," says Vitalini, who redesigned the space. "Every detail is to my liking." With chequerboard floors, green velvet upholstery and Thonet chairs, it's an appealing space for a morning cappuccino or evening pinot noir: the doors stay open till 23.30. In 2022 the café started making its own gin with Fishers distillery in the UK, as well as backgammon boards with French company Hector Saxe. "I like to try different things," he says.
belmontstmoritz.com

CAFÉ
COFFEE PAGE
Lausanne

Lausanne's first café-library, established in 2019, combines speciality coffee with art books. "The culture of café-libraries is rooted in France, where cafés are intrinsically linked to a culture of literature," says founder Jean Kehlhofer. "In Switzerland, we're less accustomed to combining the two." Kehlhofer took great care over the address's airy aesthetics. In the evenings, Coffee Page transforms into a bar offering a fine whisky selection (whisky being Kehlhofer's third obsession after coffee and design) and cocktails. There are distillations from Scotland, Japan, Sweden and Finland, with cheese, cured meats, and bread from cult bakery Bread Store.
coffee-page.com

CAFÉ
APFELGOLD
Berne

Donat Berger (*pictured, on left*) baked his way to success by hosting *schnouse* every other Wednesday in his home. This Bernese pastime, which consists of sampling sweet snacks between meals, developed into a business in 2012 when Apfelgold was born. The apple-shaped sign hanging above the entrance hints at the hero ingredient of Berger's delicacies. "When I was a kid, we had a few apple trees… we took the harvest to the cider maker, who pressed the juice for us," Berger says. At Apfelgold, you can taste apple varieties as juice, cider, non-alcoholic spritz or purée. As for the baked goods, chocolate, crème brûlée and other seasonal fruit options are on offer too.
apfelgold.ch

BAKERY

TSUGI
Zürich

BAKERY

COLLECTIVE BAKERY
Zürich

Inside a concrete pavilion next to the headquarters of footwear and sports brand On, a team of passionate bakers prepare goodies that blend culinary traditions. Experimentation is one of the core values at Collective Bakery: "We bring different experiences to our daily work and we try to exchange our knowledge and talk through every product," says baker and owner Nino Brüllmann. You might find sweet buns with seasonal fillings, pain suisse and Japanese *shokupan* arranged side by side on the counter. Yet one of the most popular products remains a famous flaky variation of a hand-rolled French croissant that sells by the hundred. *collectivebakery.ch*

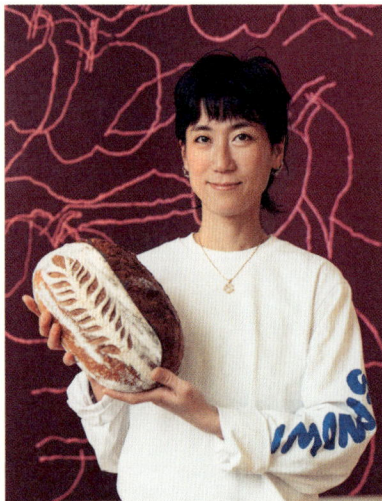

Tokyo-born Jinny Watanabe (*pictured*) learned to knead dough in Japan before setting up her Zürich bakery. "Switzerland has the advantage of high-quality produce thanks to its four distinct seasons," says Watanabe. The result is Tsugi, which combines her love for Japan's umami flavours with ancient leavening techniques, creating crowd-pleasers such as salty seaweed croissants, nutty miso *knäckebrot* (rye crispbreads) and *tamago* (egg) sandos. The contemporary *konditorei* now attracts a stream of locals hankering after fluffy *shokupan* milk bread and sourdough made from stone-ground organic Vollkorn wheat milled in nearby Glarus canton. *tsugi.ch*

MAGDALENA BÄCKEREI
Rickenbach, Schwyz

High above Lake Lucerne on the slopes of the Mythen, chef Dominik Hartmann, Adriana Hartmann and Marco Appert opened Magdalena restaurant in the summer of 2020. A few months later, the kitchen was awarded two Michelin stars. Dominik's passion for baking led the trio to add a bakery in 2021. "His breads are all sourdough and he has perfected the recipe for his Magdi bread in particular," says Adriana. Customers are also spoiled with fluffy croissants, cinnamon knots, pains au chocolat and Danish pastries, all overseen by head of bakery Andreas Camenzind (*pictured*).
restaurant-magdalena.ch

Bread for success
Magdalena's bakery is now beneath the namesake restaurant. "We had wanted to do this for a long time but first tested the project with a pop-up in the Bistro Bären in Schwyz before moving into the permanent location here," says Adriana Hartmann, who is the organisation's designer.

BAKERY
LAMIETTE
Geneva

Lamia Benmoussa came to Geneva in 2015 and
Lamiette is a riff on her first name that translates aptly
to "the crumb" in French. Unlike Geneva's traditional
bakeries that err on the unadventurous, Benmoussa
dispensed with the rustic wooden interior. Instead,
Lamiette feels clean, unstuffy and relaxed, ensuring
Gallic savoir-faire takes centre stage. Pastry chef
Antoine Lethien uses Swiss-sourced ingredients to
create buttery pain pralinés, bouncy orange blossom
brioches and effortlessly laminated pain suisse. In the
unlikely case of any leftovers, Benmoussa's canine
companion Milkyway is always happy to oblige.
Rue de Saint-Léger 5

BAKERY
GARDE-MANGER
Ardez, Graubünden

Run by brother-sister duo Rémy and Lucie Bailloux
(*pictured*), Garde-Manger stocks the produce they've
eaten since childhood. "We grew up in the French Alps
and food was always important," says Rémy. You'll
find pastries made by Lucie, who studied pâtisserie in
France, but also other delicious pantry fillers. Although
many of these kitchen essentials can be kept for months,
seasonality is still key to the shop's ethos. Villagers
and visitors pack its Café La Carsuot for lunch, which,
when in season, serves game hunted by Rémy. For
the siblings, serving dishes that reflect the region's
delicacies and variety is what sets them apart.
garde-manger.ch

HANSELMANN
St Moritz

Frosty days in St Moritz call for a visit to Hanselmann café and confectionery shop for a pastry and hot chocolate with cream. The business has spanned four generations from 1894, when Fritz Hanselmann and his wife, Theresia, opened their own bakery. Today, Hanselmann's cakes and treats are made fresh daily from traditional recipes. Residents and tourists alike travel for a taste of the Engadine nut cake and St Moritz snowballs: white chocolate truffles with milk praline filling and a little Grand Marnier. Also on offer are buttery pastries and soft breads, promising something for every craving. *hanselmann.ch*

Chocolate-box exterior
Hanselmann has hosted everyone from King Farouk of Egypt to author Thomas Mann. In the centre of town, the building has an exterior clad in wood panelling with a pattern of rosettes and hand-painted frescoes.

IN FOCUS
CHOCOLATIERS
The art of the delicious

Melt-in-the-mouth diplomacy
Swiss confectionery is much more than just a luxury product – it's a diplomatic tool. No world leader leaves Switzerland without a box of pralines, while business conferences are frequently conducted over beautifully packaged confectionery. Swiss chocolate remains an example of sweet soft power that proves difficult to resist.

Banks and watches showcase Switzerland's precise, discreet efficiency but chocolate is the nation's third superpower. When Rodolphe Lindt invented a new stirring method in Berne in 1879, he revolutionised the texture of chocolate, making it melt-in-the-mouth and creamy for the first time. It was the start of a global success story for Swiss chocolate. Zürich institutions Sprüngli and Honold are among the most renowned manufacturers in the country. Founded in 1836, Confiserie Sprüngli sets the benchmark with its buttery pralines and Grand Cru varieties. Confiserie Honold, a traditional Zürich chocolatier since 1905, delights with handmade truffles. Auer is a fixture in Geneva, having been established in 1939. Since its opening, customers have been delighted by the high cacao content in its products. Bernese chocolate manufacturer Tschirren should not go unmentioned – it has been synonymous with first-class Swiss confectionery for three generations. Today, young labels such as Laflor and Garçoa from Zürich or Xocolatl from Basel are forging new paths, focusing on industry transparency, sustainability and bean-to-bar craftsmanship. New manufacturers are also experimenting with rare cocoa varieties and innovative recipes showing a return to quality and authenticity that is redefining chocolate culture.

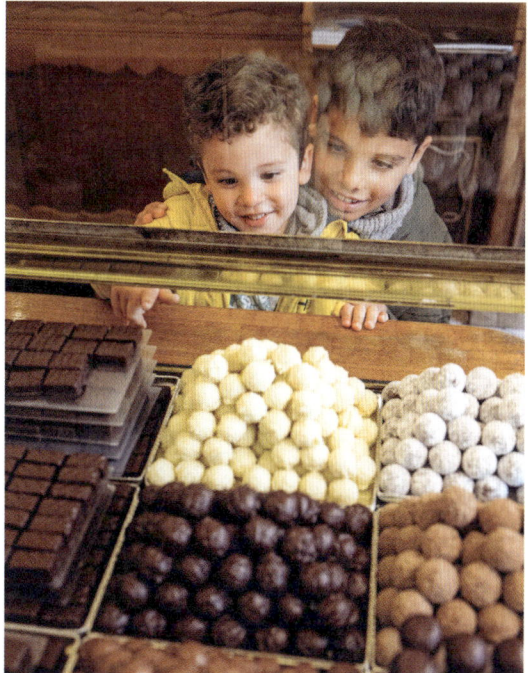

1   A selection of chocolate treats at Auer
2   Auer headquarters in Geneva
3   Auer chocolate almonds
4   Inside the Xocolatl shop in Basel
5   Spoilt for choice at Auer
6   Sprüngli shopfront in Zürich
7   Xocolatl owner Maren Gnädinger

FROMAGERIE
WILLI SCHMID
Lichtensteig, St Gallen

Willi Schmid (*pictured*) savours milk like others do wine. "Only healthy soil gives good grass and only good grass results in good milk," he says. This milk allows him to produce varieties such as his jersey blue, a cheese made from yellow jersey milk. "The milk comes with the highest cream level so I don't need to add more," he says. It will make great bergfichte – a creamy, almost runny variety ripened in spruce bark. While his cheeses are widely available in fromageries across the country, his fresh jersey butter and fondue are exclusively sold in his shop in Lichtensteig. And with a little luck, you can watch the cheesemaker at work through the window.
willischmid.ch

FROMAGERIE
LA MAISON DU FROMAGE STERCHI
Neuchâtel

This family-owned business has cultivated a passion for cheese since 1928. The fromagerie is in the medieval old town of Neuchâtel with stone walls and wooden beams framing the shop's interior. Inside are shelves showcasing aged truckles and counters stacked with neatly labelled wedges. Stocking 70 to 90 varieties, depending on the season, the shop specialises in Swiss Alpine cheeses such as Jura gruyères and chaux d'abel. International cheeses are also available, should you want to indulge in goat and cow varieties from France or Italy. A selection of wines are also offered – the perfect reward after a day of exploring.
sterchi-fromages.ch

FROMAGERIE
MOLKEREI GSTAAD
Gstaad

Wheels of fortune
Visitors are welcomed to the underground grotto where the Bernese Alpine AOP cheese is left to age. "In here we store about 30 tonnes of cheese," says managing director René Ryser (*pictured*). Each wheel must be stored underground for at least 18 months, with the most mature being about 90 years old.

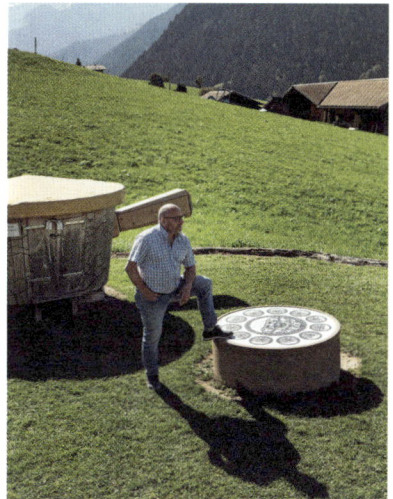

Molkerei Gstaad (or "Gstaad's dairy farm") has been crafting exquisite Alpine cheeses since 1931, courtesy of the town's commitment to mountain farming. In the heart of Gstaad, at Molkerei you will find wedges of traditional mountain cheese infused with Alpine meadow herbs, velvety rounds of tomme florette handmade in Rougemont and full-bodied edelweiss cheese native to the resort town. There's even a refrigerated cheese vending machine outside the premises, Gstaad's solution for when the dairy cravings kick in out of hours.
molkerei-gstaad.ch

FOOD RETAILER
JUCKER FARM
Seegräben, Zürich

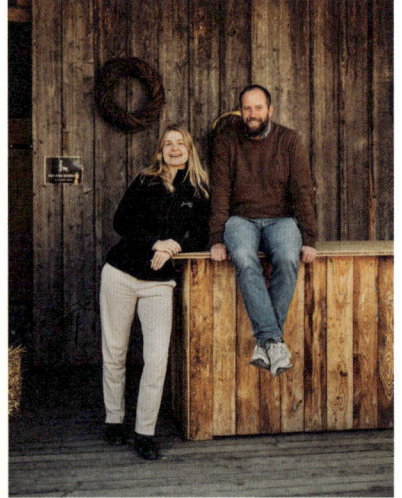

In the village of Seegräben on Lake Pfäffikon, Jucker Farm's Juckerhof location is run by Reto Benker (*pictured, on right*) and home to a restaurant, bakery, farm shop, goat petting zoo and pick-your-own produce. The Jucker family's adventure farm came to fruition in the 1990s, starting with Juckerhof and a pumpkin exhibition (that still draws visitors every autumn) and later expanding to three other farm shops across Switzerland. The restaurant offers a filling breakfast and there is a big brunch buffet at weekends. Inside the shop is an array of produce as well as a selection of flavourful condiments and fresh bread baked in the on-site bakery.
juckerfarm.ch

FOOD RETAILER
H SCHWARZENBACH
Zürich

This historic old-town establishment has been selling hard-to-find spices, ground coffee, tea and condiments since 1864. Its comely wares range from sun-ripened dried fruits and rich chutneys to organic pasta. However the shop is perhaps best known for the fresh coffee it roasts in-house and its selection of flavoursome teas. There is no self-service at H Schwarzenbach: an astute, uniformed team advises customers on each product. This dedicated staff and old-world ambience of H Schwarzenbach suggest little has changed since the store opened – and that has proven to be a very good thing.
schwarzenbach.ch

BOTTLE SHOP
NINO
Geneva

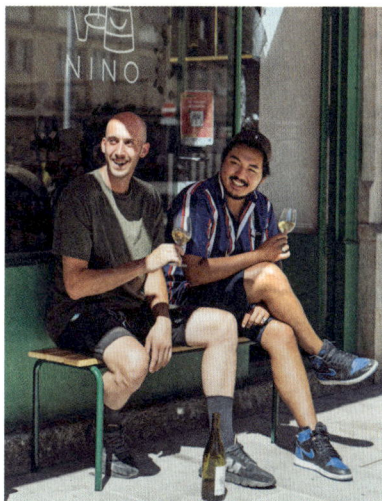

In Geneva's Jonction quarter, Nino is a laid-back wine cave selling the best natural and biodynamic varieties. It was opened in 2020 by friends Vincent de Ferluc and Anand Batdelger (*pictured, on right, with De Ferluc*), who met while working at the nearby Birdie café. "I am French, and in France there is a *caviste* in every neighbourhood in every city," says De Ferluc. Nino offers tastings and events featuring winemakers both new and established, and though it sells international wines there is a focus on French and Swiss varieties. "Many Swiss winemakers make biodynamic and organic wines, with little to no added sulphites," says De Ferluc.
ninocave.com

MARKET
IM VIADUKT
Zürich

Built in 1894 as a railway viaduct, this 500-metre stretch of arches was once just a piece of infrastructure, linking train hubs in Zürich. But since its transformation in 2010, the Viadukt has become one of the city's most vibrant spaces. Beneath it is a mix of boutiques, design studios, homeware stores and culinary hotspots. At its heart is the Markthalle, a bustling indoor market offering some of Zürich's finest produce. The hall has a tempting selection of delicacies, from hand-folded gyozas to Swiss cheeses, while the adjoining restaurant is a firm favourite. The space is also a cultural hub, hosting exhibitions, live performances and community events.
im-viadukt.ch

MARKET
HALLE DE RIVE
Geneva

A culinary metropolis set back from a busy street, Halle de Rive showcases some of the best flavours Geneva has to offer. Take a stroll down the market's winding alleys to find an impressive array of local products: fresh cuts of meat, seasonal produce, artisan cheeses and delectable desserts. Under lighting provided by globe lamp posts, meticulously stocked counters are managed by local merchants who can be found sharing the origins of their products with passers-by. From expert butchers to specialist pâtissiers, there is something for every craving, palate and preference.
halle-de-rive.ch

MARKET
MARCHÉ DE LA VIEILLE VILLE DE SION
Sion

Framed by two hills, one topped with a fortified basilica and the other a medieval castle, the historic town of Sion is a charming backdrop for this weekly market. The canton of Valais is a sunny, fertile region famous for apricots, which can be found here bottled as nectar or *eau de vie* year round. Even in early spring, the farmers lay out locally grown savoy cabbage, dandelion greens, parsnips and black garlic. Nearby fromageries supply single-origin cheeses offering a richer taste than a mass-produced equivalent. With bags filled, shoppers can linger at high tables with a glass of wine or two.
mvvsion.ch

With its own distinct culinary tradition and influences from its neighbours and beyond, Switzerland has no shortage of ideas with regard to food. We ask four industry leaders what they bring to the table.

MEET THE EXPERTS

NOÉMI BERNARD
Sternen Walchwil

Sternen Walchwil in the picturesque village of Walchwil on the banks of Lake Zug is a historic inn and family business. Chef Noémi Bernard runs the establishment's restaurant with her parents, Giorgio and Anita, and creates dishes with fresh ingredients and refined aromas.

How much are you inspired by the nature of the canton of Zug for your cuisine?
I put a strong focus on cooking in tune with the season and whenever possible I use regional produce. So whatever is available on the market and whatever the season offers me sets the pace. They are the parameters within which we create the dishes in the kitchen.

What is your favourite Swiss flavour or product?
I can't pick one. I love herbs, fruit, mushrooms and dairy products from our village of Walchwil. We have many cherry blossom trees in the region of Zug, so I long for the cherry season every year. Across the lake is the Boog family in Hünenberg and I make sure not to miss their exceptional strawberries.

Is it special to you to work alongside your parents?
We are a family business and lead the restaurant with heart. Since we are so close, communication is very direct and it makes it very easy to work together.
sternenwalchwil.com

DISTILLERS
GIAN AND FLORIAN GRUNDBÖCK
Deux Frères

BAKER
HIRONORI TAKAHASHI
Hiro Takahashi

Brothers Gian (*pictured, left*) and Florian Grundböck (*pictured, right*) founded distillery Deux Frères in the canton of Zürich, combining their inventive spirit and love for a good drink. Starting with a gin based on 25 botanicals, they went on to produce a vermouth, a rosé and a sparkling wine. At their Zürich-based site they offer tastings and insights into their craftsmanship.

What inspired you to create Deux Frères?
When we started in 2016, there were only a few Swiss gins and nothing that really felt exciting. We recognised a gap in the market and knew that we could create something new. Our backgrounds are in business and food engineering and we had this strong inner urge to create something of our own.

What inspired you to develop an alcohol-free sparkling rosé?
Our vision from the very beginning was to create products with an exceptional flavour. And this goes well beyond producing a good gin. We see ourselves as a brand for moments of pleasure, so we continue to develop drinks with flavour and quality – with and without alcohol.

What do you enjoy most about your work?
We are living our dream. As brothers we have a great relationship, our sister is also part of the company and our wider team is fantastic. We love working with inspiring people and bringing our creative ideas to life.
deuxfreresspirits.com

Hironori Takahashi bakes Japanese-style breads and sweet treats in his bakery near Zürich for local businesses, including the Monocle Café (*see page 69*). After moving from Japan to Switzerland in 1999, Takahashi worked as pastry chef in the Savoy Hotel for eight years, before opening his bakery in 2009.

Why did you come to Switzerland?
I am the fourth generation of a family of bakers that has been operating in Niigata for 100 years. While attending culinary school in Japan, I discovered my love for baking bread and wanted to learn European methods. That's why I moved to Switzerland.

Where do you find inspiration for your products?
I make classic Japanese pastries. In the past, I adapted my products to Swiss tastes but in recent years so many Swiss people have visited Japan and enjoy authentic Japanese flavours that I no longer need to make adjustments. My style combines European products with Japanese influences, such as a roulade with yuzu and matcha. Nowadays, people even come to me with recipe suggestions and I do my best to bring them to life.

What makes your products special?
I import many of my ingredients directly from Japan. One of my bestsellers is the melon bun, a sweet bread covered with a vanilla biscuit layer in the shape of a melon, because melons were a luxury item in Japan. But the most important thing is to create products with heart and motivation – customers can feel that too.
hirotakahashi.com

Switzerland's entrepreneurs have long used the country's fine tradition of quality artisanship to bring life to their ventures. For flowers to fashion and furniture, here are our choices of the best places to go shopping.

DESIGN & RETAIL

The Swiss take pride in well-made, functional objects, which makes any shopping safari here a joy. A visit to Switzerland is a great opportunity to visit flagship stores of heritage brands that have perfected the manufacture of knives, watches, skis and sledges for decades – if not centuries. We'll also take you off the beaten track to meet the finest purveyors of handwoven towels, embroidered tableware and chic footwear. And should you be in need of a bespoke suiting service, we'll leave you in the capable hands of the couturiers from our time-tested address book. Local shopkeepers have honed their craft and product selection for generations to delight their discerning clientele. Many of them cultivate relationships with international brands and complement Swiss classics with Japanese antiques, South Tyrolean mountain apparel, Czech stationery, modern Indian furniture or Taiwanese accessories. So how much space do you have in your suitcase?

THE EDIT

1 **Retail**
If you need to refresh your wardrobe, then look no further.

2 **Specialists**
Our list of Swiss companies that are the very best at what they do.

3 **Watches**
The epitome of quality, precision and accuracy and one of Switzerland's most famous specialities.

4 **Furniture**
If you're looking for handsome items to sit on, look at or rest your coffee mug on, this is where to go.

5 **Concept stores**
Stores with an art-inspired approach to selecting (and making) their wares.

6 **The experts**
Swiss entrepreneurs talk about their inspirations and experiences.

RETAIL
THE APARTMENT STORE
Zürich

Ideal home
The high-quality fabrics and inter-seasonal selections on offer at The Apartment Store are key to its success. The top floor also offers a collection of items from past seasons offered at lower price points, welcoming deal-seekers to this multi-floor treasure chest too.

Multi-brand shop The Apartment Store is home to a number of Swiss and international labels, from Kiner ceramics to knitwear specialist Wommelsdorff and contemporary womenswear brand Claudia Bertini. It opened its doors in 2004, when founders Hanspeter Limacher and Marcel Hofmann (*pictured*) had the ambition of putting together an establishment that would introduce Zürich to a variety of international brands. Visitors to the shop can find timeless designs, colourful fabrics and accessories such as Bea Mombaers leather handbags and Common Projects shoes.
theapartmentstore.ch

TRUNK
Zürich

Mats Klingberg founded Trunk in 2010 with a vision: to create the kind of menswear shop he wished existed. Drawing inspiration from Japan and Italy, Swedish-born Klingberg wanted to move away from impersonal stores and instead offer a warm, welcoming space. Trunk focuses on timeless menswear that blends smart and casual, allowing customers to build a wardrobe with ease. It also prioritises service, without the pressure of commission-driven sales. "Trunk is a place of discovery, where customers can find new things they haven't seen before," Klingberg says. "It's not about the newest or the trendiest but about quality, craft and things that last."
trunkclothiers.com

Brand leader
Trunk's philosophy has helped the shop establish itself as a unique retail destination. The Zürich store, opened in 2018, is the second – the first was in London. Another key part of Trunk's identity is its in-house brand, produced in Italy, Scotland and Portugal.

RETAIL
MAKING THINGS
Zürich

RETAIL
QWSTION
Zürich

This bright three-room shop in the city's colourful Langstrasse neighbourhood offers a selection of clothing, jewellery and accessories. It was founded in 2005 by textile and fashion designers Clod Bernegger and Hanna Kawasaki, who met while working for a creative agency and decided to sell their own designs and printed creations. Today the store's racks and white-painted tables are lined with items made in Switzerland, Europe and Japan. The range includes Spanish brand Cordera, Sweden's Maska and Japanese hat maker Chisaki. In 2014 the duo – who are both mothers – opened the child-focused Making Little Things in the residential area of Kalkbreite.
makingthings.ch

Born out of a mission to revolutionise the textile industry, Zürich-based label Qwstion offers something different. Each bag is made from plants instead of plastic. Having developed a biodegradable banana-fibre textile, the brand's regenerative vision is captured in its high-quality products. Qwstion's mission also extends to the shop floor. "We wanted to create an atmosphere that allows customers to take their time to dive into the story behind our bags," says co-founder Christian Paul Kägi. With experienced team members keen to share the brand's story, visitors can browse sleek, minimalist bags, all-weather coats and other accessories all in good conscience.
qwstion.com

RETAIL

RETAIL
ENSOIE
Zürich

Ensoie started out as a silk-trading company in 1894
and was taken over by Monique Meier in the 1970s.
Today it's in the hands of Meier's daughters Sophie
and Anna (*pictured, on right, with Sophie*), who together
have given the brand a fresh lease of life. The sisters
have brought a new type of cool to the label and
expanded the customer base from 40 to 60-year-olds to
20 to 30-somethings. The store has other locations in
Altstadt and Basel but this five-storey flagship in a 14th-
century building has the largest selection of the brand's
homewares, as well as cheery dresses, hand-woven
scarves and coats.
ensoie.com

RETAIL
VIU
Basel

RETAIL
BLANCHE
Basel

In keeping with Switzerland's most coveted brands, Viu subscribes to the sleek Swiss aesthetic, creating glasses with functionality and minimalism in mind. The frames – designed in Zürich and made in the Italian Dolomites and Japan – are characterised by pared-down patterns, sleek shapes and neutral tones. The shop, opened in 2013, is a combination of beauty and practicality. Wooden beamed ceilings and exposed brick frame the crisp white space, while glasses perch on modern shelving. "We wanted to create a space that seamlessly blends the city's historic charm with Viu's contemporary design ethos," says co-founder and creative director Fabrice Aeberhard. *shopviu.com*

The clothes at Blanche, found just off Basel's central Marktplatz, have what founders Anita Moser and Sabine Lauber (*pictured, on right, with Moser*) call *ecken und kanten*. It's a phrase that literally means "corners and edges" but is used as a metaphor for their collection's distinctive and individual design. Lauber and Moser stock a mix of Swiss designers: "It's a very personal selection," says Moser. The pair maintain links with local universities and partner with new designers to guide them through the process of working with boutiques and building a label, while Blanche also repairs and refreshes leather and knitwear in an atelier above the store. *blanchestudioshop.ch*

PELIKAMO
Berne

Solid foundations
"The Swiss like solid things: a solid house, a solid car and solid clothes," says Vadasz. Quality is therefore favoured over frills. Pelikamo's wares are made in Italy, Portugal and Switzerland using materials from established fabric houses such as Loro Piana.

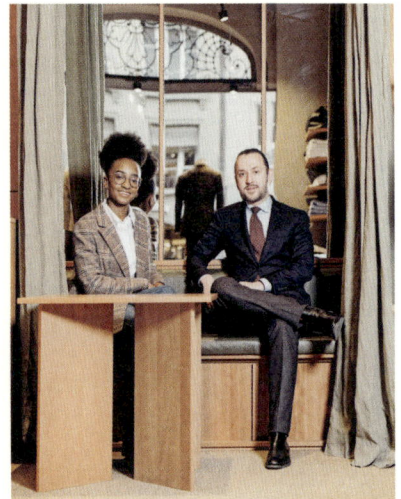

Although Zürich-based, this menswear brand now has outposts in Berne and Basel that dress bankers and urban professionals day and night via its bespoke suiting service. Pelikamo is conservative in its aesthetic – and sensibly so. Inside, there are chunky knits alongside inky-blue chinos, crisp cotton dress shirts and brown leather loafers. Sebastiaan Vadasz and his wife, Mia Vadasz, co-founded Pelikamo in 2011 and since then the label has become a popular choice for well-made Swiss menswear, attracting a loyal clientele that admires its quality.
pelikamo.com

ZWAHLEN-HÜNI
Saanen, Berne

"From the start we wanted to provide our customers with a curated retail experience," says third-generation owner Philipp Zwahlen (*pictured*) of Zwahlen-Hüni's 1948 formation. "It's a philosophy we maintain to this day." The multi-brand boutique mainly sells German and Austrian *tracht* (traditional) brands such as Bavaria-based Poldi and Mirabell Salzburg but there are also cardigans by Italian label Gran Sasso, knitwear by Luisa Spagnoli and cashmere by Doriani, plus leather brogues by Crockett & Jones. Services like home delivery, tailoring and personal advice are key to Zwahlen-Hüni's success. "Our customers will always find something special with us," says Zwahlen. *zwahlenhueni.ch*

PESKO
Lenzerheide, Graubünden

In the charming resort town of Lenzerheide, fourth-generation retailer Pesko boasts an impressive collection of skiwear and sports equipment. Established in 1901 by shoemaker Franz Konrad Pesko, it became the town's first sports shop and today sells and rents out technical gear for winter and summer sports. In the company's store, established in 1989, there are three floors displaying a selection of thermo-sensitive jackets from Italian luxury house Stone Island, South Tyrolean mountain apparel by LaMunt and trainers from Swiss brand On. There's even a contemporary art gallery and espresso bar on the top floor to make the shopping experience into an occasion.
pesko.ch

ATELIER TREGER
Lucerne

Couturier Anna de Weerdt and menswear specialist Markus Elmiger started handmaking braces in their living room in 2009. Since then, the braces have been a mainstay, each pair unique and hand-finished. The collection, however, has diversified: there are now bow ties and pocket squares, as well as mens and womenswear from delicate vests and well-cut chinos to crisp linen shirts and bespoke suits. All the pieces are designed by the duo and are made with high-quality materials from European mills. Fittings are an integral part of the experience, with the goal being to "show clients how well-fitting clothes can change their lives", says Elmiger.
treger.ch

RETAIL
GIOVANOLI SPORT & MODA
Sils Maria, Graubünden

Known for its tall peaks and lush valleys, the Engadine has attracted hikers and skiers for more than a century – and Giovanoli Sport & Moda has been outfitting them in the village of Sils Maria since 1949. Now run by Annigna Giovanoli (the third generation of Giovanolis) and her husband, Reto Hungerbühler, the shop still supplies sporting gear and outerwear but has adapted to the demand for après-ski attire by stocking contemporary fashion brands such as Claudia Bertini, Petar Petrov and Silvano Sassetti. The shop itself is minimalist and bright with white walls and hardwood and stone floors. Ski and snowboard equipment is also available for rent.
giovanoli-sils.ch

RETAIL
MONSIEUR ALAIN
Geneva

Monsieur Alain is a trove of simple, quality menswear on Geneva's Boulevard de Saint-Georges in trendy Plainpalais. The shop offers brands including Orslow, Arpenteur, Sunspel, Paraboot and Portuguese Flannel with every item selected by a team led by Alain Dovat. Working with the Red Cross to establish clothing stores in Geneva gave Dovat a first taste of retail entrepreneurship. The initial Monsieur Alain location opened in Lausanne in 2013, followed by a second in Geneva. "We believe that what you wear should align with how you live," says Dovat. "We appreciate craftsmanship, a job well done, beautiful fabrics and attention to detail."
monsieuralain.ch

MAISON LORENZ BACH
Gstaad

In 1978 ski-instructor Lorenz Bach decided to change tack and open a winter sports shop in his native Gstaad. At the time there was little in the way of high-quality fashion in Saanenland. "I stocked luxury sportswear brands such as Bogner and Moncler because I wanted to bring couture to Gstaad," says Bach. As he attracted well-heeled holidaymakers, fashion giants followed suit, profiting from the appetite for luxury fashion cultivated by Bach. Today you'll find a goldmine of more than 150 niche labels. There are leather totes from Hogan, suede loafers by Santoni and flannel shirts from Artigiano alongside Bach's namesake collection of prêt-à-porter.
lorenzbach.ch

AVART
Lugano

Avart your eyes
Just a few steps from the picture-perfect Lake Lugano, Avart spans two beautifully designed retail spaces. In the womenswear section, marble and travertine details complement softly textured walls, while oak panels, raw concrete, industrial steel and *kukido*-style floral arrangements set the tone in the menswear space.

Avart's well-stocked shelves come from close relationships with a broad range of designers, brought together by founder Alma Veragouth (*pictured, on left, with collaborator Giacomo Veragouth*). Veragouth is originally from Kazakhstan and the daughter of a tapestry artist. Her selection reflects her understated style and interest in textile craft. You'll find *trompe l'oeil* jewellery by Maria Sole Ferragamo, handbags by interior stylist and designer Bea Mombaers and elegant wool coats by Lilia Litkovska. Avart is proof that the brick-and-mortar shopping experience can't be replicated online.
avart.ch

VICTORINOX
Zürich

SÜSKIND
Zürich

With precision and functionality, fêted knife, watch and travel-gear maker Victorinox is the pioneer of the patented Swiss Army Knife. Founded in 1884 by Swiss cutler Karl Elsener, the company designed its iconic creation with soldiers in mind. The idea was to create a screwdriver, can opener, blade and reamer in one multi-purpose pocket tool that has since become a global symbol of national soft power. Current iterations include a wood saw, scissors, pliers and bottle opener and the brand has also branched into household knives and travel apparel, meaning Victorinox's logo remains a potent representation of Swiss practicality.
victorinox.com

Mayumi Matthäus (*pictured*) has always been fascinated by perfumes. The Zürich native travelled the world as a Swissair flight attendant and would pick up different scents and labels wherever she went. "I'd find niche brands that I had never heard of and you would never see in Switzerland," she says. In 2012 she opened Süskind (named after writer Patrick Süskind, who wrote the 1985 novel *Perfume*) in a 300-year-old building in the city's Altstadt. While she stocks some big names, Matthäus tries to carry lesser-known brands. "It was always important to find brands that were really small and artisanal," she says. "I like to know the story behind each scent."
sueskind.ch

SPECIALIST
FABRIKAT
Zürich

The motto "working goods for good working" aptly sums up the nature of the objects stocked by Zürich-based retailer Fabrikat. The stationery, household goods and workshop tools emporium carries a timeless selection of goods including desk organisers custom-made in the canton of St Gallen and Japanese toolboxes, as well as pencil pots made in the Basque Country and Czech mechanical pencils. But there are also German multitools and French aluminium pepper mills sitting on well-stacked shelves among enamel kitchen essentials, paper glue and garden secateurs.
fabrikat.ch

Objects of desire
Fabrikat's philosophy prioritises skilled craftsmanship and small-batch manufacturing, creating a veritable cornucopia rooted in a steadfast Helvetic pride over well-made and functional everyday objects.

SPECIALIST
MARTIN GROSSENBACHER BLUMEN
Zürich

Budding entrepreneur
Grossenbacher comes from a family with a deep love of flowers and was surrounded by blooms from an early age. There were always fresh flowers in the house and beautifully arranged pots outside. After training as a gardener, he continued his education to become a florist, opening his corner shop in 1997 and turning his lifelong passion into a profession.

Since 1997, Martin Grossenbacher (*pictured*) and his team have been providing the highest-quality flowers in Seefeld. His shop is known for its vibrant and diverse selection, offering flowers in all colours and following the seasons when possible. The floral industry has evolved in Zürich and independent producers have become rare, while sustainability has gained importance. However, the love for flowers remains unchanged. "A flower is never trendy; a flower is simply always beautiful," says Grossenbacher. Bright and colourful bouquets are as popular as ever, he adds, and beautiful in every season. *martingrossenbacher.ch*

SPECIALIST
POPPY
Geneva

In Geneva's Plainpalais, Poppy's storefront stands out in white and green, framed by flowers and potted plants that spill onto the pavement. Yann Popper (*pictured*, *below right*), who grew up in Geneva, opened it during the pandemic when flower shops were exempt. "I'm not a florist but it was the only thing you could open," he says. When restrictions eased, Popper began selling to local restaurants and the business grew. Today it is a jungle-like space and among the wilderness live two fish called Simon and Gaston (named by Popper's daughter), four canaries and two lovebirds, whose warbles emanate from the greenery. *poppyshop.ch*

STÖCKLI
Malters, Lucerne

Based in Malters, a 20-minute drive from Lucerne's city centre, Stöckli is the only remaining ski manufacturing facility in Switzerland. The origins of Josef Stöckli's ski business come from the late founder's penchant for experimenting with new and innovative ski construction techniques. Starting with wooden skis created in his parents' carpentry workshop, these evolved into metal skis and eventually the top-notch plastic compound iteration we're familiar with today. Producing more than 75,000 pairs of skis per year, the brand remains determined to continue manufacturing its products by hand in Switzerland.
stoeckli.ch

LINDAUER
Schwyz

In this sporty region of the Swiss Alps, the name Lindauer is synonymous with the finest (and fastest) sledges on the slopes. "Most people going down the mountain have been overtaken by a Lindauer at some point, and then they come to us," says Jo Lindauer (*pictured, with daughters Viola on right and Medea seated on sledge*), who began in traditional carpentry before turning to sledges at his family's Schwyz-based shop in central Switzerland. "I inherited the workshop from my father, who inherited it from his father." With his daughters, Viola and Medea, Lindauer makes about 200 sledges each year, as well as some 70 toboggans.
lindauerschlitten.ch

TESSANDA
Santa Maria Val Müstair, Graubünden

Tessanda is one of Switzerland's last remaining weaving mills. "We are an important cultural asset for the Santa Maria Val Müstair municipality," says managing director Maya Repele (*pictured*). The mill uses natural yarns including flax and silk, mostly sourced from local traders. Each item has a small label featuring the weaver's name that speaks to their originality. Created using antique weaving looms, its textiles focus on homeware and tableware as well as carpets, embroidery and towels. Tessanda's handmade textiles ensure this form of artisanship is stitched into the Engadine's cultural heritage. *tessanda.ch*

The thread of history
Since its inception, Tessanda has remained a female affair with a women-led team ensuring that the traditional craft is both preserved and promoted. It was founded in 1928 by two handicraft teachers with support from pastor Rudolf Filli, because women were not allowed to sign contracts or open bank accounts at the time. Fida Lori, one of the founders, later took charge of the mill.

CASHMERE HOUSE LAMM
St Moritz

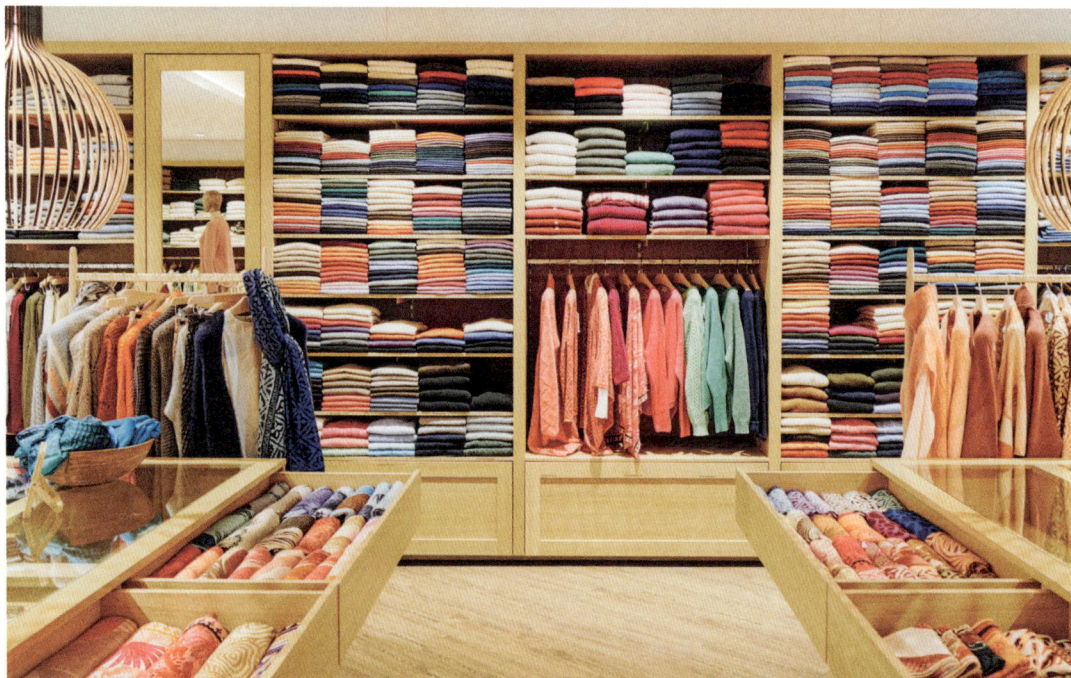

On St Moritz's Via Maistra, the Lamm family has been selling items to shield against the cold for more than 90 years. The business was originally opened by saddler and upholsterer Luzian Lamm and sold everything from sledges and skis to gear for horses and outerwear for Alpine conditions. Today the shop offers the finest cashmere knitwear, mostly made in Scotland and Italy. "We're a classic shop; I don't like to carry styles for just the season," says Natascha Lamm, who took the reins from her father in 2011. With the child-focused Little Lamm now open next door, they cater for all ages. "Cashmere jumpers don't go out of style," says Lamm. *cashmerelamm.ch*

SPECIALIST
EBNETER & BIEL
St Moritz

This family-owned hand-embroidery and home textile business has been producing quality linen since 1880, originally in Appenzell, a region known for its embroidered textiles: it later set up shop in St Moritz's Badrutt's Palace (*see page 43*) in 1911. Today the shop is found on the Plazza dal Mulin in the centre of St Moritz and is run by the fourth generation – Christian and Andrea-Rita Biel. "Everything is made by hand and it's important we know where everything comes from," says Christian. For this reason the siblings have chosen not to expand the business or hire other staff, believing customer service is best left to the family.
ebneter-biel.ch

DISCOVER SWITZERLAND | SPECIALIST

IN FOCUS
WATCHES
Time waits for no one

Turning back the clock
Where there are watchmakers, there must also be master restorers. In Geneva, that place is Horlogerie Desbiolles, a quietly revered atelier founded in 1986 and now run by the second generation of the Desbiolles family. This workshop not only restores timepieces with forensic care but also offers a selection of vintage treasures.

Switzerland remains the undisputed heart of watchmaking – a landscape where time is not just measured but meticulously crafted. Steeped in centuries of precision, master horologists hone their skills with unwavering dedication, passing down time-honoured techniques while embracing innovation. High in the Vallée de Joux, where the craft of watchmaking has endured for centuries, Bulgari has carved out an unexpected niche. It's here, in this Swiss cradle of haute horology, that the Roman house renowned for opulent jewellery and architectural boldness has quietly become a force. Vanguart also emerges as a beacon of avant-garde innovation. Founded in 2017 in La Chaux-de-Fonds, this independent Swiss maison melds traditional craftsmanship with futuristic design.

Tucked into the elegant shopping streets of Geneva, Zürich and Lucerne since 1964, Les Ambassadeurs has curated an array of timepieces from the world's most prestigious maisons. Inside, polished vitrines gleam with Blancpain, Omega and Breguet. Meanwhile, Jim Gerber offers a curated collection of vintage wristwear at his own Zürich establishment. As a master watchmaker, Gerber ensures that each watch is restored to its original integrity. His commitment to exemplary quality makes this boutique a haven for discerning collectors of IWC, Longines, Breitling and Rolex.

4   5

6

1 Bulgari Swiss manufacturing HQ in
  Le Sentier
2 An eye for detail at Bulgari
3 Vanguart watch in its rightful place
4 Haute horlogerie at Bulgari
5 Bulgari watches on display
6 Thierry Fischer, creative director at
  Vanguart
7 Pascal Legendre, head of Bulgari's
  Grande Sonnerie atelier

7

FURNITURE
H100
Zürich

H100 is a furniture store that serves as home to three specialist shops in Zürich West and has become a destination for design enthusiasts since it opened in 2019. The concept brings together Bogen33, with its mix of vintage pieces and garden furniture; Viadukt*3, known for solid wooden tables and chairs; and Memorie.ch, which offers re-editions of design classics from the 1930s to the 1980s alongside contemporary European furniture. Just 100 metres away, the Openstorage warehouse contains an extensive collection of mid-century finds and one-off gems housed in a former underground garage. Visitors can browse Bauhaus armchairs, timeless dining sets and playful garden chairs, displayed both inside and outside. "We sell furniture with essence; with history and ecological meaning. We restore and refine each piece, supported by a workshop that we've had since the beginning," says founder Fabio Dubler. H100 is both a treasure trove for collectors and a practical stop for anyone looking to furnish their home with character.
h100.ch

CONCEPT
LIMITED STOCK
Zürich

CONCEPT
GRIMSEL
Basel

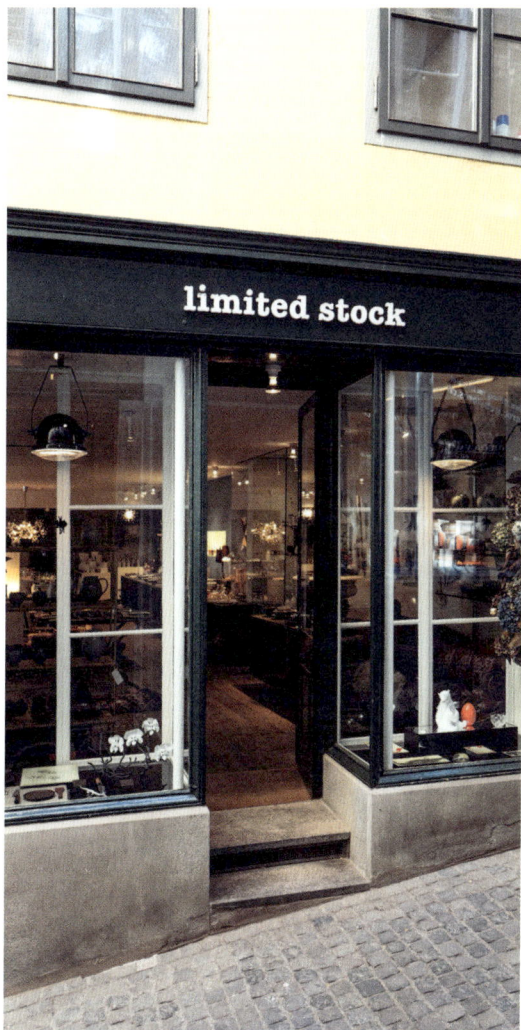

Grimsel is a tranquil place to browse, featuring brands such as Karimoku Case and Embru, alongside textile murals, original prints, ceramics and vintage pieces. "Care and quality in design and workmanship are the basis of all our products," says graphic designer and co-owner Alexa Früh, who with interior architect Bettina Ginsberg opened the showroom overlooking the Rhine in 2014. Grimsel is also an interiors studio that offers consulting, colour, furnishing and styling services. The duo are particularly fond of their in-house line, Serie Grimsel, which includes plush cushions, soft throws, leather accessories, sleek stools, cupboards and shelves. *grimsel.net*

This chamber of curiosity does what it says on the tin: here, stock is limited because sculptor Hubert Spörri and interior designer Ulrich Zickler have chosen a portfolio of brands that only produce in small batches. The duo sources from workshops in Europe and Japan and brings antique rugs and fabrics from Morocco and the Middle East, creating a cornucopia of objets d'art. Popular offerings are handblown Viennese glassware from Lobmeyr, metal Japanese tea tins from Kaikado and functional German ceramics from Keramische Werkstatt Margaretenhöhe. "It's quite a strange mixture but it's one you won't find anywhere else," says Spörri. *limited-stock.com*

CONCEPT
TEMPO
Lausanne

Setting up shop in the Swiss Alps in 2017 was a result of the many travels of business partners Pablo de Pinho and Ana Deffarges. "It's rare to find lifestyle shops with a smart international selection in Switzerland," says De Pinho. "We knew Lausanne was missing something." The result is a collection featuring items from furniture ateliers including Copenhagen-based Frama and Bangalore's Phantom Hands. There are leather goods from Tokyo's Hender Scheme and wicker from Taiwan's Kamaro'an, plus menswear from École de Pensée. The showroom itself is an inviting space with hardwood floors, large windows and Scandinavian lighting and furniture.
tempodesignstore.com

CONCEPT
KITCHENER
Berne

This legendary retail outpost on Aarbergergasse is steeped in underground culture. Opened in 1967 by Eva and Jürg Huber (with Heinz Mischler), their daughter Sarah Huber is now at the helm and the family business continues to thrive. Brands such as Toast, Soeur and APC, as well as home-bred label Kitchener Items are on show across the 680 sq m space, which also displays homewares and premium pantry supplies. The owners take pride in the wide selection of items that are sold in their shop: "We even recently started selling plants because I'm a keen gardener," Sarah says. "We do whatever we find fun."
shop.kitchener.ch

ROOM
Klosters, Graubünden

SUPER MOUNTAIN MARKET
St Moritz

Berliner Mario Weichselmann and jewellery designer Angelo de Luca sought to combine culture, artisanship, design and cuisine in their Super Mountain Market concept shop, so you'll find Gliva 01 healing balm made from local herbs, Alva knitwear crafted from natural fibres and Yali Glass produced in Murano. The store collaborates with the likes of Handformwerk, South Tyrol-based atelier Rier and Paris-based Art Noble gallery, with items by emerging brands such as Henriette Leimer and Rosi Kahane also on sale. Good coffee was vital to the vision and, with beans roasted locally, Super Mountain Market's café promises exactly that.
superstmoritz.com

Room is a family-run business started by Anita Hew (*pictured*), working with her daughter Anna and son Felix. "What makes Room special is that it's truly a family effort," says Anita. "We know Klosters by heart and together we've created something that feels both cared for and carefully considered." The store offers a thoughtful blend of international brands in fashion, jewellery and design. With an integrated café-bar, the space feels more like a meeting point than a shop and it is frequently used for local events such as concerts, exhibitions and gatherings. "We see it as an intimate space where you can enjoy a matcha in the morning or a glass of wine as the day winds down."
Bahnhofstrasse 13

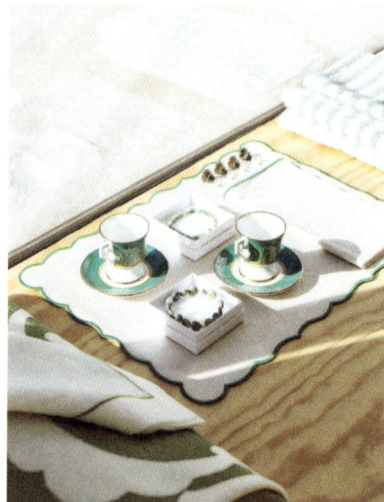

Switzerland is renowned for its precision engineering and chocolatiers but the nation's tradition of artisanship goes much further than this. We talk to three modern practitioners.

MEET THE EXPERTS

FASHION ENTREPRENEUR
NOËLE NANA SCHAFFNER
Nomadissem

Swiss-born Noële Nana Schaffner worked in marketing and business management before moving to New York to study at the Parsons School of Design. She launched Nomadissem in 2020. We asked her about the inspiration and concept behind her Zürich-based brand.

How did you decide to start your own fashion label?
I wanted to do something on my own, something in fashion. In 2015, I was travelling a lot but always packing the wrong things. Essentials were always missing. I came up with this idea of having a wardrobe where you mix and match so you can throw in a few things and when you get to your destination everything fits with each other.

How does the quality of materials factor into your business?
The main idea is that you can keep the garments for a lifetime and pass on to future generations. For that you need good materials and you need good craftsmanship. I start from the materials and then from there I design.

What was the biggest challenge of starting your own brand?
In the beginning it was hard to find the right suppliers. I finally found ateliers in the north of Italy. I think it's important that you come across people who believe in your idea and in your concept and help you realise what you really want. Don't let people dilute your idea.
nomadissem.com

DESIGN & RETAIL

DESIGNER
INI ARCHIBONG
Design by Ini

WATCHMAKER
SANDRINE DONGUY
Vacheron Constantin

THE EXPERTS · DISCOVER SWITZERLAND

Ini Archibong is a California-born designer with Nigerian roots. Archibong moved to Switzerland in 2014 and founded his own design studio Design by Ini in 2010. He is known for his range of artfully crafted designs (from furniture to watches) for brands such as Hermès, Knoll and Sé and his work has been displayed at galleries and museums including The Met in New York.

How has Switzerland inspired and influenced your work?
I came to Switzerland to study and one of the major things I learned and that inspired me to stay was the level of Swiss craftsmanship. After graduating from École Cantonale d'Art de Lausanne (ECAL), I travelled by train all over the country meeting craftsmen and I began building the network. In that sense the designer that people know me as today is completely shaped by Switzerland.

Would you say Switzerland is a good base for designers?
I think there's a reason that certain things thrive in Switzerland from a design and creative standpoint and it has a lot to do with the beautiful views we have and the peace and quiet. Things work, things are on time and, because of that, you have less to distract you.

How do you create something for a brand while staying true to your own philosophy?
It's not that difficult for me to do because I've been fortunate enough to work with brands I share an identity with. My philosophy, especially when it comes to commercial work, is to make sure that these objects carry a quality within them that gives them a value that's beyond their functional usefulness.
designbyini.com

Vacheron Constantin, the world's oldest continually operating watchmaker, has a steady hand on heritage and a clear eye on innovation. At the centre of that balancing act is Sandrine Donguy, the maison's director of product and innovation.

Vacheron Constantin marked its 270th anniversary in 2025. How do you innovate without losing sight of your heritage?
Our starting point is always our roots, whether it's the Maltese cross, an openworked dial or the way we finish a calibre. That identity gives us freedom to take measured risks. We dare but with elegance: never ostentatious, always a touch of quiet audacity.

Which recent launches best illustrate that balance between tradition and forward-thinking?
The relaunch of the 222 has been hugely significant; it answered a demand from collectors while staying true to its original spirit. At the other end of the spectrum is our astronomical complication, which allows the wearer to track constellations in real time. It's poetic and technical, and shows how we merge innovation with emotion.

Beyond design and mechanics, how is the maison preparing for the future of watchmaking?
Longevity is at the core of our philosophy. We've introduced solar panels at our facilities and developed a certified pre-owned programme that restores and recirculates archival models at the highest level. At the same time our apprenticeship schemes ensure savoir-faire is passed down at the bench. A mechanical watch is more than a tool: it's personal, emotional, enduring and that's why it will remain relevant for centuries to come.
vacheron-constantin.com

We've compiled a round-up of our favourite Swiss products to help you pick out your ideal purchases – from cast-iron fondue sets to excellent chocolate and fiendishly clever wooden toys.

THE SHOPPING LIST

1. Deux Frères rosé
   deuxfreresspirits.com
2. Lahco retro beach bag
   lahco.ch
3. Ann-Kathrin Kuhn Sous le
   Soleil bracelet
   annkathrinkuhn.com
4. Drogerie Meer Herbarium
   body oil
   drogerie-meer.ch
5. Sprüngli choc-oranges
   spruengli.ch
6. Jucker Farm apple rings
   juckershop.ch
7. Atelier Volvox forest glasses
   ateliervolvox.ch

1 Chien Bleu cider
   chienbleu.ch
2 Ensoie tote
   ensoie.com
3 The Cocktail Zürich negroni
   thecocktail.eu
4 Sprüngli Zürcher leckerli
   spruengli.ch
5 Seifenmacher orange spice soap
   seifenmacher.ch
6 Studio Sediment espresso cup
   and saucer
   studiosediment.com
7 Original Fish scampi stock
   original-fish.ch
8 Honey dill mustard sauce
   from Pernet Gstaad
   pernet-comestibles.ch

1   Cuboro wooden marble-run toy
    cuboro.ch
2   Rivella drink
    rivella.ch
3   Michel Charlot tap tumblers
    michelcharlot.com
4   Gold Ölmühle apricot oil
    goldoel.ch
5   Carrack Grand Cru chocolate bars
    carrack.ch
6   ZigZagZurich blanket
    zigzagzurich.com

1 Zürischum Blau brut
   zurischum.ch
2 Kuhn Rikon cast-iron fondue set
   kuhnrikon.co.uk
3 Pepe Valle Maggia pepper
   pepevallemaggia.ch
4 Gruyere vieux AOP
   kaseswiss.com
5 Züri Senf mustard
   zuerisenf.ch
6 Sula tray
   sulaworld.com
7 Goodlife Ceramics coffee cups
   goodlifeceramics.ch

DISCOVER SWITZERLAND | THE SHOPPING LIST

1 Caran d'Ache watercolour pencils
   carandache.com
2 Michel Charlot O-Tidy by Vitra
   vitra.com
3 Victorinox Swiss Army Knife
   victorinox.com
4 Trauffer wooden goat
   shop.trauffer.ch
5 Ensoie tablecloth
   ensoie.com
6 Sirocco beef stock
   sirocco.ch

7 Ovomaltine cocoa
   ovomaltine.com
8 Carnet Numéro notebook
   carnetnumero.ch
9 Trendform matches
   trendform.com
10 Valotsavons milk soap
   valotsavons.ch
11 Thomy mayonnaise
   nestle.com

1 Jucker Farm tomato pumpkin sauce
juckerfarm.ch

2 Poschiavo pizzoccheri
pastificio.ch

3 Original Fish lobster broth
original-fish.ch

4 Original Fish fish broth
original-fish.ch

5 En Bocal salted butter caramel spread
enbocal.ch

6 H Schwarzenbach trietolt powder
schwarzenbach.ch

7 Meat Design peperoncini in agrodolce
meatdesign.ch

8 Siroscope ginger and orange blossom syrup
siroscope.ch

9 L'Elefantino ceramic plate
lelefantino.ch

10 Deux Frères dry gin
deuxfreresspirits.com

11 L'Elefantino ceramic bowl
lelefantino.ch

1 Pasta Bonetti wild garlic tagliatelle
  biopastabonetti.ch
2 Kindschi Röteli cherry liqueur
  kindschi1860.com
3 Adank pinot noir
  adank-weine.ch
4 Park Books 'Drifting Symmetries'
  park-books.com
5 Fabrikat scissors
  fabrikat.ch
6 Ghilli Plage Paloma body bar
  ghilli.ch
7 Fabrikat glycerine soap
  fabrikat.ch
8 Bally Ribbon bifold wallet in black
  grained leather
  bally.com
9 Blumer glarner tüechli scarf
  blumer-f.ch
10 Ebneter & Biel St Moritz
  cocktail napkin
  ebneter-biel.ch
11 Longines Conquest Heritage watch
  longines.com

1   Al Canton Ida G herbal tea
   al-canton.ch

2   Odur fragrance
   odur.ch

3   Ledibelle rich moisturiser
   ledibelle.ch

4   Soeder lavender field natural lotion
   soeder.ch

5   Label17 laptop case
   label17.com

6   Bulgari Serpenti Tubogas watch
   bulgari.com

7   Laflor dark chocolate
   laflor.ch

8   The Soap and the Sea eucalyptus
   and sea salt soap
   thesoapandthesea.com

9   Drogerie Meer signature moon oil
   drogerie-meer.ch

The Swiss nation is home to some of the most respected cultural institutions in the world. Here is our selection of the places to enjoy the country's most impressive collections and most inspiring experiences.

CULTURE

Switzerland has an abundance of world-class museums, spanning painting, sculpture, design and even horology. Yet it's also worth perusing the rich cultural calendar before you travel to ensure you're not missing out on events such as the charming Locarno Film Festival or the legendary Montreux Jazz Festival. The success of Art Basel proves that Switzerland knows how to put on a show: first launched in the 1970s, it was the brainchild of three local gallerists and has put this Swiss city on the map for the world's collectors, curators, creatives and artists. There are many charming galleries outside of the cities too, including exhibition spaces in quirky locations such as a former cowshed in Klosters or transformed railway workers' lodgings in Vevey. We'll also introduce you to the entrepreneurs who are keeping the nation's print and publishing heritage alive and show you extraordinary historic cinemas renovated to their original splendour. Curtain up!

THE EDIT

1 **Museums**
The best of the nation's hallowed historical repositories.

2 **Galleries**
Spaces where you can experience Swiss visual arts up close.

3 **Cultural centres**
Multi-disciplinary spots playing host to a variety of events.

4 **Cultural events**
Art festivals in stunning landscapes with precise Swiss organisation.

5 **Music venues**
Handsome spaces wired for sound.

6 **Cinemas**
Beautiful temples dedicated to the glamour of the silver screen.

7 **Bookshops**
Attractive and dynamic shops devoted to the printed word.

8 **Publishers**
Some of Switzerland's sharpest, most innovative presses.

9 **The experts**
Three cultural leaders give us their thoughts on the state of Swiss art.

MUSEUM
FONDATION BEYELER
Riehen, Basel-Stadt

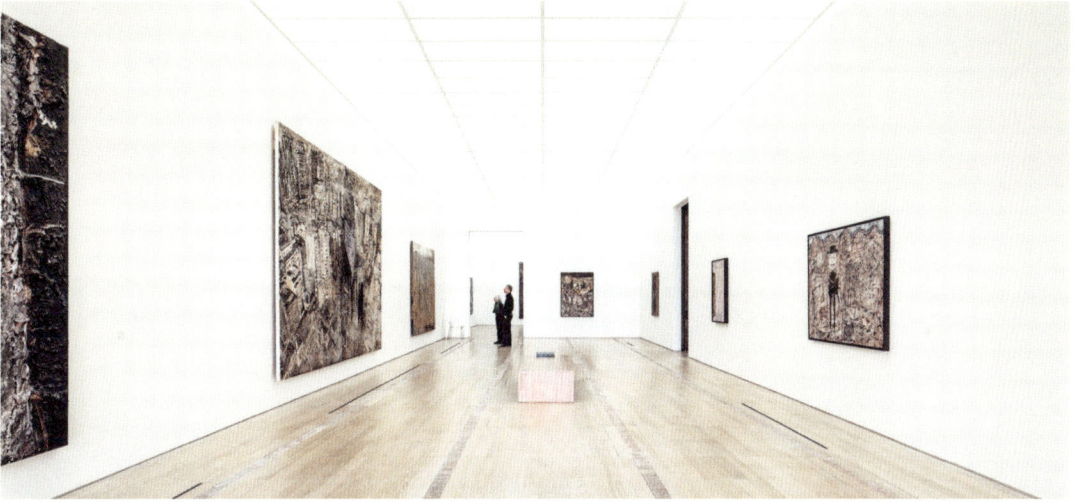

In 1997, art dealers Hildy Beyeler and her husband Ernst opened the doors to Fondation Beyeler in their hometown of Riehen, just outside Basel. They intended for the space to house their impressive art collection of 19th, 20th and 21st-century masterpieces. Today, more than 400 works of impressionist, classic modern and contemporary art occupy the building. Open all year, the centre hosts talks with renowned artists, music performances, art workshops and even a mobile studio located in the park, which offers inspiration and materials for creative exploration of the environment. *fondationbeyeler.ch*

Light fantastic
The Fondation Beyeler building was designed by Italian architect Renzo Piano. With its floor-to-ceiling windows and glass roof, the museum space is filled with natural light and scenic views and overlooks the surrounding landscape of old trees and water lily ponds. The restaurant in the premises' park serves dishes from the region's culinary heritage.

MUSEUM
KUNSTHAUS ZÜRICH
Zürich

Kunsthaus Zürich emerged in 1787 from the humble beginnings of a small group of artists who traded drawings among themselves. Today the museum attracts more than half a million visitors every year. The immense collection includes both public and private works: from icons of impressionism to relics from the middle ages. The resulting worldly, era-spanning selection has both local and international allure. Multi-language tours and private workshops helmed by experts are available and at the end of an art-fuelled afternoon visitors can head to the inviting Kunsthaus bar.
kunsthaus.ch

(Partially) private collection
In 2021 another building – designed by David Chipperfield – was added to the Kunsthaus Zürich campus, making it the largest art museum in Switzerland. Two thirds of the works across the museum are on loan from private lenders and donors.

MUSEUM FÜR GESTALTUNG ZÜRICH
Zürich

Holding more than half a million objects, the Museum für Gestaltung Zürich is home to Switzerland's largest design collection and gives recognition to the nation's record of fine design and craftsmanship. The museum reimagines the design of everyday objects, such as Alessandro Mendini's colourful caffettiera (a redesign of Bialetti's Moka Express pot) and inventor Alfred Neweczerzal's Rex vegetable peeler. "Our programme endeavours to convey the enormous importance of design in a fun and exciting way, inspiring as many people as possible," says director Christian Brändle (*pictured*). *museum-gestaltung.ch*

MUSEUM

KUNST MUSEUM WINTERTHUR
Winterthur, Zürich

Beyond the doors of the Kunst Museum Winterthur, visitors will find masterpieces from the 17th century to the modern day. From early romantic paintings, realist and impressionist works to classical modern sculptures, post-war art and minimalism, the institution's extensive displays can be admired for hours on end. Among the pieces are works by Vincent van Gogh, Jean-Etienne Liotard and Claude Monet, as well as part of the Oskar Reinhart Collection. Spread across three buildings, exhibits can be enjoyed between walks through the surrounding greenery and stops in nearby cafés. *kmw.ch*

Park life
Once the beating heart of Swiss industry, Winterthur is now host to some of the nation's finest galleries and museums. Much of the city's cultural life now plays out before a backdrop of verdant parks.

MUSEUM
ZENTRUM PAUL KLEE
Berne

For the ultimate Berne cultural fix head just outside the city to the Zentrum Paul Klee: this interdisciplinary cultural centre – dedicated to the Swiss-German artist born nearby – focuses on painting but there are other creative forms on show too as visual art is often combined with music, literature and more. Designed by Renzo Piano, the wave-like glass-and-steel structure holds the world's largest collection of works by the 20th-century master. There are 4,000 items, with a permanent collection and rotating thematic shows, and the venue also stages exhibitions of modern and contemporary names, from Picasso to Bridget Riley.
zpk.org

MUSEUM
L'APPARTEMENT
Vevey, Vaud

On the second floor of the former railway workers' lodgings at Vevey station, this unassuming hub has exhibited contemporary photography since 2021. The viewing experience takes place in two apartments measuring 220 sq m. "We carried out the renovations in such a way as to maintain the atmosphere and characteristics of these domestic living spaces," says director Stefano Stoll. Staged as a residential space, *Le Salon* features book-related projects, *Le Couloir* hosts displays positioned at a child-friendly height, *Les Chambres* houses monographic exhibitions and *Le Cinéma* offers an immersive corner for visitors to take in digital content.
images.ch

MUSEUM

CERN SCIENCE GATEWAY
Geneva

Cern Science Gateway allows visitors to engage closely with the discipline. Guests can experiment in workshops, peruse exhibitions, view shows in the auditorium and visit labs. The building is designed by Renzo Piano Building Workshop and Brodbeck Roulet Architectes Associés, and symbolises the link between science and society: the tubular building emulates Cern's accelerators, while glass-lined corridors represent a determination to make science accessible to the public. The building is also carbon-neutral, solar-powered and in a forested area, reflecting a commitment to sustainability. Science-themed drinks and a bite to eat are available in the restaurant. *visit.cern*

MUSEUM

MUSÉE D'ART ET D'HISTOIRE
Geneva

The Museum of Art and History is housed in a palatial building in the Vieille Ville, designed by Swiss architect Marc Camoletti at the turn of the 20th century (although the museum itself dates back to the 19th century). The museum's encyclopaedic collection includes some 650,000 works, largely composed of donations and bequests from the city's inhabitants, ranging from historic portrait miniatures and local archaeological finds to rare books, sculpture and fine art. As a tribute to the community that has built the institution, concerts, DJ sets and workshops are also offered to the public year-round. *mahmah.ch*

MUSEUM

MUSÉE ATELIER AUDEMARS PIGUET
Le Brassus, Vaud

Overlooking the Jura mountains in the Vallée de Joux, the Musée Atelier Audemars Piguet stands on the site where founders Jules Louis Audemars and Edward Auguste Piguet originally set up shop. Today, it houses more than 300 significant timepieces from the maison spanning two centuries, alongside two ateliers where artisans craft each piece by hand. Designed by architecture studio BIG, curved glass walls frame panoramic views of the snow-capped surroundings and the space takes the form of a spiral, where tours follow a clockwise route, symbolic of a watch movement.
museeatelier.audemarspiguet.com

Time and space
At the centre of the building, the Grandes Complications Atelier is where watches are decorated, adjusted and cased by expert hands. The front of the atelier, inspired by the solar system, hosts a constellation of historic timepieces displayed in spherical cases orbiting around the Universelle, one of the most complicated wristwatches the brand has ever produced.

BERNHEIM
Zürich

LARKIN ERDMANN
Zürich

Larkin Erdmann founded his gallery in 2014 and moved it to its current Altstadt location in early 2025. The gallery focuses on around 20 artists, predominantly from the period 1940 to 1960. Each exhibition is accompanied by a meticulously crafted catalogue, designed not just as an event companion but as an enduring record. "The exhibition disappears," says Erdmann, who is also a collector and dealer, "but the catalogue remains." With just three to four shows a year, the gallery remains intentionally small and has become a key contact point for collectors interested in figures such as Max Bill, Alighiero Boetti, Alberto Giacometti and Man Ray.
larkinerdmann.com

The buildings on Zürich's Rämistrasse have a salon-like air that's completely different to the industrial-chic warehouses found in the west of the city. Maria Bernheim opened her eponymous space there in 2015 and is one of the area's less conventional gallerists. Her ambitious location reflects her radical art curation – passers-by double-take when they walk past her windows showing the darkly comedic Russian sketcher Ebecho Muslimova or absurdist Chinese artist Ding Shilun. "Some might not like what they see," says Bernheim. "But I like the friction." The gallery's 2023 expansion to London shows that this unconventional approach clearly works.
bernheimgallery.com

EDITION VFO
Zürich

Handsome prints
Edition VFO visitors can expect to
encounter exclusive prints by up-and-
coming artists, as well as pieces by
leading contemporary figures such as
Wade Guyton. Be sure to peruse the
gallery's standout works, including
Renée Levi's monumental monotype
and the *Scarch* portfolio by Swiss
artist Not Vital, before exploring the
institution's vast archive.

Edition VFO is a gallery, publisher and arts institute housed in
the Löwenbräukunst arts centre. Placing printmaking at the
heart of its mission, Edition VFO collaborates with renowned
and emerging artists to showcase the best of the medium.
"Visiting Edition VFO is about discovery," says managing
director David Khalat (*pictured*). "Visitors leave with a deeper
appreciation for the medium and for contemporary art
production." Every exhibition is a collaboration between the
artist and production specialists, and the resulting works are
published as limited, signed and therefore valuable editions.
edition-vfo.ch

GALLERY
ATELIER BOLT
Klosters, Graubünden

Bolt action
Completed in 2016 with a wood-
pannelled sculpture studio, painting
studio and exhibition hall, Atelier Bolt
has hosted Le Corbusier's prints and
the works of Swedish artist Marianne
Bergengren, among numerous others.
It also hosts seminars and workshops
for international students.

Uster-born sculptor and painter Christian Bolt (*pictured*) has
created a vibrant cultural hub in his beloved Klosters, turning
a cowshed into a space for his interdisciplinary work and guest
showcases. Known for playfully interpreting classic Greek
sculptural codes, Bolt is currently working on large pieces that
draw inspiration from the village's history, tranquillity and
light. "I feel an immediate and direct connection to nature
in Klosters," he says. A visit to Atelier Bolt is the chance to
discover one of Switzerland's most celebrated contemporary
artists in the village where he's lived for more than 20 years.
bolt.ch

GALLERY
HAUSER & WIRTH
St Moritz

Spanning three floors of a building owned by nearby Badrutt's Palace (*see page 43*), Hauser & Wirth's St Moritz location is a bright and refined gallery space in the heart of the resort town. It was designed by architect Luis Laplace in 2018 and features concrete materials and floor-to-ceiling windows that overlook the snow-capped peaks of the Engadine Valley. Many featured artists, from Gerhard Richter to Jean-Michel Basquiat, have had a connection to St Moritz, being either inspired by or spending time in the mountains. "Sometimes we are able to create these special projects where these works come back to where they were created," says director Giorgia von Albertini. *hauserwirth.com*

GALLERY
KIRCHGASSE
Steckborn, Thurgau

On Lake Constance in the village of Steckborn, Kirchgasse is owned and run by curator Anne Gruber. It represents 11 artists across different media and pieces include playful glass sculptures by Stefan Burger, richly coloured photograms by Chantal Kaufmann and large-format prints by Sarah Lehnerer. "We are interested in discourse about the arts and sharing moments," Gruber says. The 16th-century Haus zur Hoffnung is a striking gallery space open by appointment on Friday and Saturday. The best time to visit is during the vernissages, which often develop from friendly gatherings to convivial dinners. *kirchgasse.com*

GALLERY
VON BARTHA
Basel

Housed in a 700 sq m former car repair shop reimagined by Swiss architects Lukas Voellmy and Chasper Schmidlin, Von Bartha has been championing modern art since 1970. Prominent Basel-based gallerists Margareta and Miklos von Bartha started the project but today the gallery is under the direction of second-generation art dealer Stefan von Bartha and his wife Hester Koper, who took the reins in 2008 with international ambitions. Von Bartha is one of few galleries to have participated in the Art Basel fair (*see page 138*) since its inception: its founders shared a stand with Hungarian-Swiss dealer and collector Carl László for seven years before presenting independently in 1978.
vonbartha.com

GALLERY
WILDE
Geneva

With outposts in Zürich and Basel, Wilde is a treasured favourite among artists and art enthusiasts. Founded by Barth Pralong and Sébastien Maret, the gallery is a contemporary art cornucopia. The flagship gallery can be found in central Geneva and inside the historic building the sweeping exhibition halls showcase projects over two spacious floors. From brightly coloured acrylic works and photography to sculptures and laminated prints, the collection is eclectic and refreshing. Beyond, guests can explore La Petite Librairie, a space devoted to artists' books, then stop at Anouch Restaurant, an inviting place where art and gastronomy mix.
wildegallery.ch

FONDATION OPALE
Lens, Valais

Following a number of encounters with artists in Australia in the early 2000s, French-born Bérengère Primat became hooked on art by indigenous Australians. Today she owns one of the largest private collections of its kind in Europe and heads up Fondation Opale in Lens, near the resort town of Crans Montana. The mission of the foundation has been clear since its inception in 2018: to help indigenous Australian art reach a wider audience. "What we want to do is to show that indigenous Australian art is at the same level as the rest of contemporary art," Primat says.
fondationopale.ch

Dreaming big
Alongside her own curatorial concepts, Primat has forged partnerships with the Yves Saint Laurent Museum in Marrakech and Tate Modern in London, proving the clout of her art centre operating from its Alpine outpost. The gallery opened a new wing in 2023, which includes a 124-seat auditorium and a library.

DISCOVER SWITZERLAND | GALLERIES

CULTURAL CENTRE
LAC LUGANO ARTE E CULTURA
Lugano

Positioned moments away from panoramic views of Lake Lugano, LAC boasts an impressive roster of music, theatrical performances and art exhibitions for site- specific shows. The multi-disciplinary hub was designed by Ivano Gianola and established in 2015, when it was the largest urban intervention in the city of Lugano. It still feels like a statement and has transformed the region into a destination for national and international audiences. The lakefront building spans 29,000 sq m and its hall is bound by glass walls that allow natural light to enter, adding to its unique flair. *luganolac.ch*

Back in LAC
Among the performers at the centre are the resident Orchestra della Svizzera Italiana, as well as Compagnia Finzi Pasca, who enrich the schedule with acrobatics, circus displays and opera. Alongside the ensembles, the venue is used for educational purposes handled by LAC edu, which engages visitors in art and culture through talks, workshops and masterclasses.

CULTURAL CENTRE
PLATEFORME 10
Lausanne

This former rail repair depot is now home to three museums (the MCBA, Mudac and Photo Elysée) and two art foundations (Toms Pauli and Félix Vallotton). Over its 25,000 sq m – including the vast Toms Pauli Foundation textiles collection and more than 10,000 artworks in the MCBA – the site combines design, art and photography, providing distinct spaces for each. The location is populated with modernist buildings from architecture firms such as Barozzi Veiga and Aires Mateus and also has places to eat, meet and relax, such as the centre's own Café Lumen, serving morning brews and craft ciders later in the day.
plateforme10.ch

IN FOCUS
CULTURAL EVENTS
Arts in the open air

In 1970, three Swiss art dealers came together to host an international mix of galleries, art publishers and visitors in their home city of Basel. That event has become the world's leading art fair and the original version has had to be rechristened to the not-so-succinct "Art Basel in Basel", given the fair's expansion to Miami, Hong Kong, Doha and Paris. The success of that endeavour is characteristic of Swiss prowess when it comes to finding new ways of bringing people together around the arts. Many of the country's cultural events are viewed as best-in-class around the world.

The younger Nomad art fair, often held in St Moritz, also offers contemporary art and design in interesting, ever-changing venues. Here you can expect cutting-edge aesthetics and fine views. Heading west, the annual Locarno Film Festival has utilised the picturesque Piazza Grande to screen films alfresco every year since 1946. Further west still, the Montreux Jazz Festival is held every summer on the shores of Lake Geneva. Over the years, it has played host to all manner of icons – Miles Davis, Ella Fitzgerald and Prince among them. Although it's no longer exclusively focused on jazz, soul and blues, the festival continues to bring in big names to perform against a pretty (and perfectly Swiss) backdrop of jagged mountains and bright blue water.

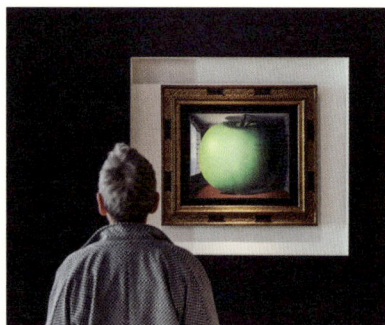

I

All that jazz
The Montreux Jazz Festival was first held in 1967 at Montreux Casino on the shores of Lake Geneva. Unfortunately, fire gutted the venue in 1971 after a blaze erupted during a concert by Frank Zappa and the Mothers of Invention, an event immortalised in the Deep Purple song "Smoke on the Water". The casino reopened in 1975 and although no longer the main venue, it still hosts shows for the festival.

2

3

1 Looking around at Art Basel
2 Nice day at the Locarno Film Festival
3 Locarno at night
4 Gathering a crowd at Montreux
5 The Art Basel whirlwind
6 This way to the Nomad art fair

4

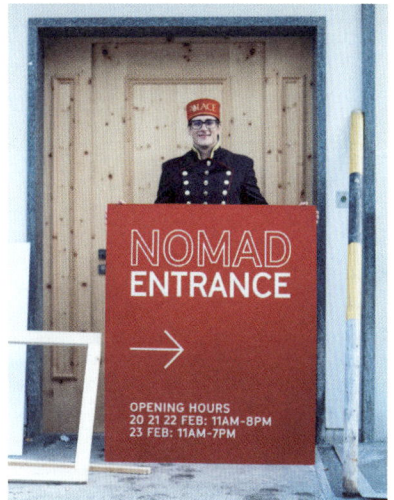

5   6

MUSIC VENUE
MOODS
Zürich

From September to June, Moods is Zürich's top spot for jazz, blues, funk, soul and everything in between. It features different artists or groups each night, with afterparties on Fridays and Saturdays (jazz jam sessions are on Wednesdays). "The intention was to have a place to perform, connect and build a community with a shared passion for music," says booker Yunus Durrer. "It has always been a mix of local artists and international musicians on tour." The space has an air of timeless cool: located in a former shipbuilding hall, Moods is famously versatile and can feel like an intimate space or mid-size venue depending on the performance.
moods.ch

CINEMA
SCALA
St Moritz

The Scala movie theatre has been entertaining viewers for nearly a century and is now one of the Engadine valley's last remaining screening venues. The sleek art deco building has become an emblem of Swiss cinema culture. The centrepiece of the space is a slide that runs from the second floor, through the foyer to the basement – upstairs guests will find a museum dedicated to bobsleighing, complete with a replica Cresta Run. The screening room is equipped with the latest technology but retains an old-school aesthetic with its 107 roomy crimson seats. There is also a restaurant, rounding out the Scala experience from cultural to historical to culinary.
scala-stmoritz.ch

CINEMA
CAPITOLE
Lausanne

Switzerland's largest cinema offers an experience reminiscent of the golden age of film. Capitole reopened its doors in 2024 after its third renovation since the 1920s and the project saw original art deco features restored with both cinephiles and design lovers in mind. "We had the opportunity not only to salvage the building but to restore it," says Marion Zahnd, one of the project's lead architects. Capitole boasts intricate 1950s chandeliers and new corrugated-aluminium walls. The screening room – which was lined with crimson velvet in 1959 – has been left untouched and a 140-seat subterranean screening room now accompanies the original 724-seat auditorium. *cinematheque.ch*

NEVER STOP READING
Zürich

In Zürich's Old Town, Never Stop Reading is stacked high with books on architecture, photography, art and design. In 2017, Swiss publishing houses Park Books and Scheidegger & Spiess collaborated to open this design-savvy, independent bookshop. Today it is teeming with an eclectic mix of in-house and international works showcasing everything from Swiss culinary heritage to the age of cinema in Zürich. "This is not a bookstore where you come to look for something," say co-managers Urs Schilliger and Thomas Wyss. "This is where you come to find something." The light-filled interior is inviting: it often hosts book readings and doubles as an event space.
neverstopreading.com

HOCHPARTERRE BÜCHER
Zürich

As Switzerland's only dedicated architecture bookstore, Hochparterre Bücher is serious about its selection and its shelves are lined with more than 3,000 titles. The shop is independent but is linked to *Hochparterre* architecture magazine (the largest of its kind in Switzerland) and the associated publishing house. "There are a lot of architecture offices in Zürich and in this area in particular," says Valentin Moser, who has worked at the shop since 2024. "It's nice to see them meet and discuss their ideas." The space is dominated by a low, circular table that was the shared desk space for the architecture studio that designed the building.
hochparterre-buecher.ch

MUSIC SOUNDS BETTER WITH BOOKS
Lausanne

Former graphic designer and art director Dennis Moya Razafimandimby (*pictured*) founded Mosoma Books online in 2017 to sell art titles. When a space in Lausanne cropped up in 2023, he combined his appetite for print with his friends' love of records to open Music Sounds Better With Books. It contains visual art and culture publications, hard-to-find references and indie magazines from the 1960s, next to Japanese photo books from the likes of Masahisa Fukase. "Visual culture and music have always intersected. We find a similar audience tends to like art, photography, design and music," Razafimandimby says. *msbwb.ch*

PUBLISHERS
More than words

Print is alive and well in Switzerland, which has cultivated a vibrant publishing landscape with a commitment to the Swiss values of precision and quality. The industry emerged in Basel at the hands of Johannes Petri in 1488, who opened Schwabe Verlag, recognised as the world's first printing and publishing house. Later the industry hub moved to Zürich and today it is home to major players releasing quality works for global audiences. Lars Müller Publishers produces titles on subjects such as architecture, design and society, while Park Books offers a meticulously curated list on architecture. Similarly, independent publisher Diogenes is a haven for talented authors, with a wide programme of classics, art and cartoon volumes, as well as books for children – the latter an increasingly successful market.

With famous examples such as *Heidi* and *The Swiss Family Robinson*, youth literature is flourishing and houses operating in that market have created a stable and geographically distinctive publishing environment for writers and illustrators. Today, one in four children's books sold in Switzerland is from a Swiss publisher. United by a mission to uphold Swiss design standards and craftmanship, Switzerland's publishers operate in keeping with Lars Müller Publishers' famous motto: "From Switzerland to the world."

1

2

3

4   5

6

1 Philipp Keel, publisher at Diogenes
2 Lars Müller sorts his poster collection
3 Well-used work space at Lars Müller
4 Hands-on work at Lars Müller's studio
5 Müller himself
6 Lars Müller graphic designer Dafi
   Kühne's work space
7 Julie Cirelli, Park Books co-director

7

Switzerland is renowned for its engineering and diplomacy, but it has also made internationally recognised cultural contributions. We talk to three professionals about the country's vibrant modern cultural scene.

MEET THE EXPERTS

ART DIRECTOR
MAIKE CRUSE
Art Basel

Maike Cruse took up her position as director of Art Basel in July 2023, having previously worked as director of the Gallery Weekend Berlin. She speaks to MONOCLE about overseeing the fair and its role as an international platform for cultural discovery.

How would you describe the art scene in Basel?
Basel is unique. The city's institutions shape a rich art scene, from the Kunstmuseum Basel (*see page 147*) to private foundations such as the Fondation Beyeler (*see page 123*). What I love most is the energy and the dedication: at openings, you'll find museum directors, collectors and young creatives all coming together.

What advice would you give to up-and-coming artists?
Immerse yourself in art. Attend exhibitions, studio visits, talks and gallery programmes, or consider joining your local Kunsthalle or young museum association.

Why is Art Basel so important for local creatives?
Our fair and public programme, alongside collaborative exhibitions and events across the city, provide valuable exposure and connections. What truly sets our Basel show apart is the extraordinary quality of the artworks on display. It's like a temporary museum presenting what's important at this very moment in time.
artbasel.com

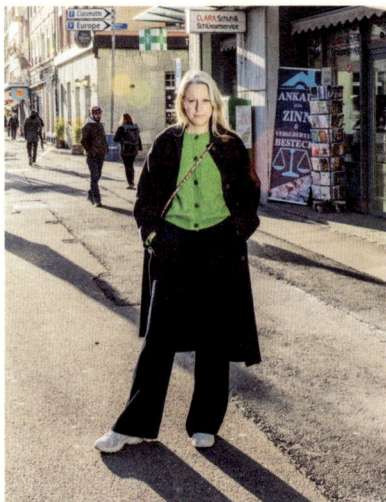

PERFORMER
PRIYA RAGU
Musician

Sri Lankan-Tamil musician Priya Ragu was born and raised in eastern Switzerland and gained international attention with her 2020 song "Good Love 2.0". We caught up with her to discuss how Switzerland influences her life and craft.

How does Switzerland influence your music?
I was raised in St Gallen, where I was constantly surrounded by local artists who organised open mics. These events played a big role in shaping my musical path. Collaborating with Swiss artists by providing backing vocals for their albums helped me grow as an artist.

Which Swiss artist inspires you?
The Swiss artist I collaborate with on a daily basis is my brother, Japhna Gold. Our shared passion for music has played a major role in shaping my sound. Another artist is Laskaar, who I have known since we were teenagers. Seeing their determination inspired me to believe that pursuing music was truly possible.

Is there a special place in Switzerland you love and think people should visit?
I recommend visiting Volkshaus in Zürich. You'll actually find me there at least once a month enjoying *fleischkäse mit bratkartoffeln* [meatloaf with fried potatoes]: it's just so good. The atmosphere, combined with the delicious local cuisine, really gives you a taste of Swiss culture that you shouldn't miss. I would also recommend Theater Neumarkt and Kunsthaus Zürich (*see page 124*). Both places are vibrant cultural hubs that showcase incredible talent and creativity.
priya-ragu.com

GALLERIST
ELENA FILIPOVIC
Kunstmuseum Basel

As the director of Kunstmuseum Basel, Elena Filipovic shapes the institution's vision – overseeing its collection, public voice and programming – and also occasionally curates exhibitions. We spoke to her about the art scene in Basel.

How has the art scene in Basel evolved in recent years?
Basel might be a small city but, thanks to art, it's always played in the big leagues. In recent years an exciting ecosystem of project spaces, experimental venues and artist-run initiatives has flourished, keeping the conversation fresh.

What do you look for when curating exhibitions for the Kunstmuseum Basel?
A museum like the Kunstmuseum Basel should be a mirror, a question mark and a provocation. It should speak to our time because art has always been a way of making sense of the world we live in. I want to highlight artists who haven't yet been fully recognised, contextualising their work and making it accessible.

Why is the Kunstmuseum Basel unique in Switzerland?
The Kunstmuseum Basel is home to the world's oldest public art collection. This deep commitment to accessibility is precisely why I wanted to lead this museum. With more than 300,000 works spanning eight centuries, the Kunstmuseum Basel is not just vast, it's alive. But what excites me most about it is the way it continues to ask what a museum can be. It carries its legacy forward as an engine for reinvention, ensuring that the past, present and future of art remain in constant conversation.
kunstmuseumbasel.ch

Switzerland contains many remarkable buildings but the fact it was the birthplace of Le Corbusier is reflected in its particularly enthusiastic adoption of modernism, as shown in this list of striking structures.

ARCHITECTURE

The transformation of rock into concrete fascinated young Jean-Luc Godard so much that he dedicated his first short film to the colossal construction of La Grande Dixence dam in Valais. Opération Béton paints a picture of ingenious engineering and the material that shaped modern Switzerland. While concrete tunnels and bridges linked remote parts of the country, the material also enabled architects to create extraordinary edifices. From brutalist churches to white cubes with rhythmic façade designs, this is the prime location to revel in the possibilities of concrete. Across the cantons, you can also see differences in vernacular architecture, including thick stone walls adorned with sgraffiti in the Engadine valley and gabled roofs with hand-carved ornamentation in Simmental. Inventive retrofits are giving life to timber barns and stone vintner's houses, which increasingly serve as covetable dwellings in addition to lending a sense of identity to the scenery. So what are you waiting for? Do come in.

THE EDIT

1 **Bündner Kunstmuseum**
Striking cube-shaped addition to a neoclassical museum building.

2 **La Tulipe**
Lab and office block with unusual forms.

3 **Chäserrugg Station**
Wooden mountaintop cable-car station built to complement its surroundings.

4 **Saint Nicholas Church**
Remarkable brutalist Alpine church.

5 **San Giovanni Battista Church**
Modernist chapel built in local gneiss stone and white marble.

6 **Schaulager Laurenz Foundation**
Deceptively simple-looking structure designed for storing and displaying art.

7 **Pavillon Le Corbusier**
The modernist master's final building.

8 **KKL Luzerne**
Glistening, metallic lakeside concert hall.

9 **7132 Therme**
Spa hotel that helped win its designer architecture's highest honour.

10 **Tamina Bridge**
Elegant bridge on the way to Bad Ragaz.

11 **The Rolex Learning Center**
Open-plan building on EPFL campus.

MUSEUM
BÜNDNER KUNSTMUSEUM
Chur, Graubünden

In the canton of Graubünden's capital, Chur, this contemporary section of the Bündner Kunstmuseum houses an important collection of Swiss (and in particular local Graubündner) art from the 1700s to today. Underground gallery spaces are topped with a street-level cuboid form clad in pale grey pre-cast concrete squares, where the collection of more than 8,000 works is exhibited. The modern extension was completed by Spanish architects Barozzi Veiga in 2016, and is attached to the original Villa Planta building, a neoclassical gem. The juxtaposition of the buildings has added a refreshing urban accent to the architectural culture of the city.

LABORATORY AND OFFICE BUILDING
LA TULIPE
Geneva

Housing the Swiss Foundation for Medical Research, La Tulipe is unofficially named after its flower-like form. The brutalist building rises from elegant, tapered columns that spread out into a floating faceted concrete support, with "petals" of candy-coloured glass that almost disappear into the Genevese sky. Built between 1972 and 1976 by Italian-Indian architect Jack Vicajee Bertoli, the sophisticated geometry of La Tulipe hints at the fact that he studied under the American master of concrete architecture Louis Kahn at Princeton, before working for Swiss architect Le Corbusier on the latter's concrete masterpiece in Chandigarh.

CABLE CAR STATION
CHÄSERRUGG STATION
St Gallen

At more than 2,000 metres above sea level, this station was built by Swiss architecture firm Herzog & de Meuron atop the Chäserrugg mountain. The simple, rectangular wooden building echoes the neighbouring barns and stables and blends respectfully into the landscape. Most construction materials were transported by cable car and built with prefabricated timber modules. The building houses both the Chäserrugg summit restaurant and the cable car station and as in traditional farmhouses a fireplace forms the central and unifying element of the interior design. Yet the most eyecatching features are the large windows framing a panorama of the Appenzell Alps.

CHURCH
SAINT NICHOLAS CHURCH
Hérémence, Valais

Saint Nicholas Church replaced a predecessor that was destroyed in an earthquake in 1946. Swiss architect Walter Förderer took the opportunity to create what many consider to be his masterpiece, completed in 1971. Perched high in the Swiss Alps in the canton of Valais – also home to the Matterhorn, which it arguably resembles – the angular white concrete structure is punctuated on the exterior with geometric interlocking cutouts and inside with a wooden pulpit, pews and accents that add a warm glow. This sculptural building is one of eight concrete churches created by Förderer across Switzerland and Germany.

CHURCH
SAN GIOVANNI BATTISTA CHURCH
Mogno, Ticino

Once a tiny isolated mountain village of just 40 inhabitants, Mogno is now famous for its striking marble and granite church designed by Ticinese architect Mario Botta. This work of architecture is simultaneously monolithic and jewel-like: built from local gneiss stone and white marble, the two materials are stacked in layers two metres thick.

The elliptical chapel is topped with a grid of clear glass panels that cast strips of light on the striped walls within. Some of Botta's most admired work can be found across the world: the Museum of Modern Art in San Francisco, a cathedral in Evry, France, and a synagogue in Tel Aviv.

GALLERY
SCHAULAGER LAURENZ FOUNDATION
Münchenstein, Basel-Landschaft

When the Schaulager Laurenz Foundation opened in 2003, Herzog & de Meuron was also working on London's Tate Modern and was about to become one of the world's most lauded architectural firms. This building, in Münchenstein, outside Basel, is one of its most striking works. The *schaulager*, meaning "viewing warehouse", is a series of spaces used for the storage and display of art, doing away with the traditional idea of a warehouse where art is hidden from view. At first, the building seems an impenetrable monolith but, inside, visitors are treated to light-filled gallery spaces and on upper levels smaller rooms present works in curated groups.

MUSEUM
PAVILLON LE CORBUSIER
Zürich

It's fitting that the swansong of Le Corbusier – one of the most celebrated architects of the 20th century, with an international roster of masterpieces – is in the country of his birth. This four-storey pavilion was conceived by the woman who commissioned it – Swiss gallerist and interior designer Heidi Weber – as an exhibition space dedicated to the work of the modernist master. It is the Swiss-French architect's only building constructed entirely of steel and glass and reflects Le Corbusier's meticulous eye for proportion, colour and sculptural drama. The building was completed posthumously in 1967, two years after his death.

KKL LUZERN
Lucerne

Lucerne Festival is an international classical music event that takes place each year during August and September. The Kultur und Kongresszentrum, known by all as KKL Luzern, is the main venue for the festival. Designed by French architect Jean Nouvel and completed in 2000, KKL's concert hall, Lucerne Hall and conference rooms reach out towards the lake, divided from each other at ground level by strips of water and united under an immense sloping roof of polished copper. It is this remarkable roof that has turned KKL Luzern into a symbol of modernity, reflecting as it does the waters of the lake from below and the shifting mountain light from above.

7132 THERME
Vals, Graubünden

In 1873, a sample of the mineral waters from the Valser spring was introduced to the world at the Viennese World Fair; more than 100 years later, this remote Graubünden mountain village is home to a masterpiece of contemporary architecture. Peter Zumthor – the Swiss architect who designed Therme Vals – received the 2009 Pritzker Prize, architecture's highest honour, largely because of the impact of the baths. Therme Vals, which opened in 1996, has since been renamed 7132 Therme. Each year, visitors flock to the Alpine canton to experience both the restorative waters and the timeless presence of Zumthor's outstanding design.

BRIDGE

TAMINA BRIDGE
Pfäfers-Valens, St Gallen

At nearly 200 metres high, the Tamina bridge is the highest arched bridge in Switzerland and one of the tallest in Europe. Stretching over the Tamina Gorge between the villages of Pfäfers and Valens in St Gallen, it was built to create an easier passage to Bad Ragaz. The two-lane overpass was designed by German firm

Leonhardt, Andrä & Partner and completed in 2017 after five years of construction. It was built to withstand wind and earthquakes, though its most lauded feature is its elegance – the high netted railings blend with the concrete design, while the narrow simplicity of the structure creates a pleasing contrast with the natural surroundings.

THE ROLEX LEARNING CENTER
Lausanne

Located on the EPFL research university campus and fitted out in steel and wood, The Rolex Learning Center is conceived as a flowing landscape. The roof and floor undulate, there's a sweeping glass façade and the interior shuns walls, stairways and corridors in favour of gentle slopes and terraces, creating an uninterrupted space.

Courtesy of Japanese practice SANAA, the organic style gently guides visitors through study areas, cafés and a library, encouraging interaction and collaboration. With few visible structural supports, a sense of openness is made immediately clear and the effect is to pull in people from all sides towards a central entrance.

Given that a large majority of Switzerland is mountains, lakes or glaciers, it is not surprising that being outside is such an attraction. Here are some of the best places to swim, ski or just get out in the open air.

THE GREAT OUTDOORS

If you find yourself at a Swiss railway station on a Friday evening or Saturday morning, you'll see droves of people geared up for an adventure, often holding skis, climbing ropes and Nordic walking poles. The Swiss adore nature and frequently explore the picture-perfect wilderness right on their doorstep. So jump on the bandwagon and dive into a secluded lake or shoot down a well-groomed slope. When travelling on services such as the Gourmino Express or Glacier Express, the journey can become the destination. The dramatic vistas of steep gorges, high-elevation mountain passes and historic viaducts are just the beginning: expect delicious fare and regional specialities freshly prepared in the onboard kitchen. Alternatively, if you're short on time and prefer to stay within the city limits, we also have a list of the best bains, badis and lidos where you can stretch out in the sun and squeeze a few dips into a busy schedule.

THE EDIT

1 **Badis**
Switzerland has no coastline but its tradition of lakeside badis – or outdoor public baths – makes up for it.

2 **Trains**
The Swiss rail network is a marvel of both engineering prowess and magnificent scenery.

3 **Ski resorts**
The skiing is only half of the appeal.

4 **Winter sports**
There are many different ways of rapidly descending a snow-covered mountain and the Swiss are good at all of them.

BADI
LIDO DI LUGANO
Lugano

Lake Lugano is between Switzerland and Italy, and Lido di Lugano's shallow beach is a prime spot for a gentle swim. While summer can feel tropical, the scenery is clearly Alpine. The lake's north bank is where you'll find its namesake town and the historic badi, designed in 1928 by the city's then-deputy mayor, Americo Marazzi.

SEEBAD UTOQUAI
Zürich

One of Zürich's oldest swimming clubs, this lakeside spot was built in 1890. One side of the complex is reserved for women, while men are on the other with a mixed pool in the middle. But it's more than just a spot to take a dip, as you can spend whole days here – we suggest having a long lunch at the on-site tapas restaurant.

BADI
FLUSSBAD OBERER LETTEN
Zürich

This *flussbad*, or "river pool", on the Limmat features a two-metre diving platform and 400-metre swimming channel. But the main draw is the current: the water is fast – and fun. Bathers jump in, are propelled along to Pier West and hop out downstream (then run back and do it all again). Going with the flow has never been so enjoyable.

BADI
BAINS DES PÂQUIS
Geneva

On a jetty with a view of Mont Blanc, the Bains de Pâquis is a summer hot spot, showing Switzerland at its most relaxed. The institution dates to 1872 and was threatened with demolition until Genevans prevented it by pushing for a canton-wide referendum. This communal spirit still persists, with events taking place year-round.

BADI
LAKE CAUMA
Flims, Graubünden

Switzerland is dotted with lakes but few are as beautiful as the emerald-hued Cauma. A two-hour train from Zürich, this spot offers a remoteness found only in the mountains. A yellow Postbus drops visitors near a funicular that takes them to the lake, where bathers can cool down and switch off (loud calls and blaring music are frowned upon here).

IN FOCUS
TRAINS
Running like clockwork

Every minute counts

For a country famous for its timepieces, it is fitting that one of the greatest icons of Swiss railways is the station clock. Each clock across the network is signalled by a central master clock every 60 seconds, which coordinates the start of each minute for accurate scheduling. So beloved is the modernist face that Mondaine sells a range of timepieces based on it, while Apple licensed the design for its iOS6 operating system.

In Switzerland, rail travel means more than just getting from A to B. If you compare Swiss transit with that in other European countries, it's clear that the Swiss are ahead in more than just punctuality and cleanliness; the network is simply better developed. One advantage is the beauty of the lines. The Gourmino Express of the Rhaetian Railway, for example, winds along the Albula Line between Chur and St Moritz over the spectacular Landwasser Viaduct and through the 6km-long Albula Tunnel, passing dozing cows and chalets clinging to steep slopes, while specialities such as *bündner capuns* and Engadine nut cake are served in elegant walnut-panelled carriages from the 1930s. Another extraordinary experience is the historic Furka steam railway, which runs between Realp in the canton of Uri and Oberwald in the canton of Valais through untouched parts of the Alps. The historic train traverses narrow gorges and winds its puffing way up mountains at altitudes of more than 2,000 metres.

Among the world's most beautiful lines are the Bernina Express, which travels from Chur past glaciers and down to the palm trees of Tirano in Italy, and the luxurious Glacier Express, which connects the mountain resorts of Zermatt and St Moritz via Andermatt. Delicious five-course menus by the panoramic windows are included. All aboard!

ZERMATT
Valais

Mythical mountains inspire and perhaps none more so than the Matterhorn. It presides over the resort town of Zermatt, where quality trumps quantity. With a sporty pace you can have a coffee in Italy in the morning, lunch in Switzerland slopeside and end with après at the Cervo hotel (*see page 19*) at the bottom of the valley run.

SKI RESORT
ST MORITZ
Graubünden

St Moritz is more than a storied resort town: skiing is king, but the Engadine valley offers world-class culture and unique activities. Snow polo, driving over the exhilarating Maloja Pass to Italy, the galleries of Zuoz, ice fishing on the St Moritzersee and even a seasonal MONOCLE shop are only a few of the diversions.

SKI RESORT
ANDERMATT
Uri

Andermatt feels like a secret. Accessed only by mountain passes or tunnels, the village has one road and one rail line, yet it is easily reached from Lucerne, Zürich, Milan and beyond. The resort offers something for everyone, from world-class cuisine to community, plus sport for experts, intermediates and even those new to outdoor fun.

SKI RESORT
VERBIER
Valais

Surrounded by 4,000-metre-high peaks and set amid glaciers, couloirs and some of the best powder in the Alps, Verbier is for skiers first and foremost. But few resorts with such serious skiing are as refined. The 164km of pistes are served by lifts that also provide access to nearly boundless off-piste possibilities.

IN FOCUS
WINTER SPORTS
It's a slippery slope

Snowy daredevils

If hauling yourself up an icy waterfall or throwing yourself headfirst down an icy channel isn't exclusive enough for you, there are other options available. For the less conventional, snow polo in St Moritz is a one-of-a-kind tournament where jockeys race across a frozen lake to score points in their opponents' goal.

One only needs to look around the hut-dotted slopes to understand that Switzerland's excellence in winter sports stemmed from a necessity to move in the mountains. The Alps cover more than half of the territory, so traders traversed perilous passes on skis long before groomed pistes became the norm, while hay was transported on sledges from high-altitude granaries before tourists whizzed down toboggan runs. When cities were engulfed in industrial-revolution smog and holidaymakers headed for the hills in search of fresh air, winter sports as we know them today took off.

Flat ice trails that loop through forests and across meadows have started to pop up and, unlike lakes, they're safe for ice skaters even in milder temperatures. If you're an adrenaline seeker, plunge down a cresta run: these vertiginous ice chutes boast 150 years of history and counting.

The addition of a privately booked mountain guide means an array of more challenging options becomes available. How about scaling a frozen waterfall with ice axes and crampons, or getting to a summit under your own steam and enjoying untracked powder on the way down? There's a plethora of activities to choose from whether you're a seasoned pro or prefer to be in the spectator seat. Mittens at the ready!

PART 02

PUT DOWN ROOTS

Perhaps you're considering staying longer – even settling permanently?
Allow us to introduce you to the country's best areas and the professionals
to enlist, plus a few people who have already made the move.

With a well-educated population, stable economy and sky-high quality of life, Switzerland is a great place to move and set up a business. Here are our ideas on where to put down roots.

WHERE TO LIVE

AUSSERSIHL
Zürich

This former Zürich red-light district and industrial area has evolved
into an up-and-coming neighbourhood for creatives and entrepreneurs,
making it a hot spot for food, culture and nightlife.

Population: 29,518 (municipal Zürich)
Closest airport: Zürich airport is 20 to
25 minutes away by public transport
Eat: Schnupf
Drink: Charlatan Restodisco
Shop: Making Things

Edgy, diverse and constantly evolving, Aussersihl (more commonly known as District 4) is one of Zürich's most dynamic neighbourhoods. Once an industrial and red-light area, it has transformed into a hot spot for the city's creative crowd, blending alternative culture with a thriving food and nightlife scene. By day the cafés and independent shops attract a mix of artists, entrepreneurs and locals, while at night the neon lights of packed bars and restaurants illuminate the streets. Charlatan Restodisco (*see page 64*) is a favourite for its laid-back atmosphere and varied menu, making it a great place to start the evening. For those looking for something heartier, Schnupf (*see page 47*) serves up well-executed Swiss dishes, with the option to stay for a drink in the same cosy setting. To round off the night, Olé Olé Bar provides an unpretentious spot for a final cocktail before heading across the street to 25hours Hotel, a design-forward stay that perfectly reflects the playful spirit of the district. Whether for a casual drink, a great meal or a long night out, this is Zürich at its most vibrant.

MOUNTAIN TOWN
SAANEN
Berne

Between three different mountain groups lies the Alpine town of Saanen,
a quiet spot where idyllic Swiss rural life continues just a few minutes
from the glamourous resort of Gstaad.

Population: 7,000
Closest airport: Geneva airport is a
two-hour drive
Eat: 16eme
Drink: La Casa Del Tabaco
Shop: Librairie des Alpages Sàrl

In the Obersimmental valley of the canton of Berne, where the Chalberhönibach stream descends from the south and merges with the Saane river, lies the mountain community of Saanen. Here, in the shadow of the 2,541-metre-tall Giferspitz and surrounded by the three mountain groups of the Bernese, Freiburg and Vaud Pre-Alps, you can experience the most diverse facets of Swiss rural life in just a few square kilometres. In the main town of Saanen, as well as in many of the neighbouring settlements, life is still tranquil – unlike in nearby Gstaad, which is also part of the municipality. In Saanen you can still find local handicrafts on sale: hand-knitted socks, for example, at Gybi on the Dorfstrasse, where food products from the surrounding villages are also sold. The Rössli in Feutersoey-Gstaad, part of the community of Gsteig (*see page 60*), never fails to impress, while the 16eme bar and restaurant in Mittelgässli is far removed from the Gstaad hype. The latter is near the Saanen railway station, which is also a stop on the iconic GoldenPass Express line.

LAKESIDE TOWN
VEVEY
Vaud

This relaxed, French-speaking lakeside town is known as 'the pearl of the Swiss Riviera'. Great transport links, a good environment for business and an inviting climate make it the ideal place to consider setting up.

Population: 20,000
Closest airport: Geneva airport is just over an hour away by car or train
Eat: Café de La Place "Chez Francine"
Drink: Céleste
Do: L'Appartement

Clinging to the northern shores of Lake Geneva in the French-speaking Vaud canton, Vevey is sometimes referred to as the "pearl of the Swiss Riviera", thanks to its picturesque Alpine scenery and vibrant cultural heritage. The former Roman settlement, 16km from Lausanne and about an hour from Geneva by train, is well-connected by Switzerland's efficient transport network, yet offers a welcome moment of calm away from the country's major centres. Vevey's microclimate is ideal for viticulture, reflected in its proximity to the Unesco-recognised Lavaux Vineyard Terraces. The town hosts the prestigious Fête des Vignerons wine festival, which takes place approximately once a generation to celebrate the town's winemaking heritage. Business and entrepreneurship is buoyant here, particularly in the food and beverage industry; Vevey has been home to the headquarters of Swiss multinational food and beverage group Nestlé since 1867. The town offers a stimulating business environment, a stable economy and a high quality of life – a perfect place to put down roots.

RESIDENCE
ZENTNER HOUSE
Zürich

In the early 1960s a Swiss couple travelled to Japan to track down
an errant Italian modernist architect. The result was a stunning
home in the hills above Zürich that remains remarkable today.

"The first time I met Scarpa, I was small enough to crawl onto his knees," says Edoardo Zentner. His Zürich home was designed by Carlo Scarpa in 1963, after Zentner's late parents tracked down the eccentric Venetian architectural maestro in Japan and persuaded him to return to Europe and design a residence that would bring a touch of *Bel Paese* modernism to a hillside above Zürich. The Zentner home is Scarpa's only built work outside Italy, triumphantly combining quality materials, expert craftsmanship and a daring form, exemplified by the cascading open-plan spaces that tier down the sloped site into the rear garden. With internal balconies, soaring cylindrical chimneys and purpose-designed furniture that complements the forms of the structure, this singular building is both a striking work of art and an intimate family home. "I could never tell you how the mind of an architect works, especially Scarpa's. However, it's perhaps not too dissimilar to the work of a great composer," says Zentner.

MENZEL APARTMENT
Saint-Maurice, Valais

Occupied by a husband-and-wife architect team, this apartment
conversion on the top floor of an 18th-century building was bound
to be something special. It doesn't disappoint.

In the small town of Saint-Maurice in the canton of Valais, Catherine Gay Menzel and her husband, Götz Menzel, reside in a spacious apartment on the upper floor of a grand 18th-century building with a view of the Alps. The couple established their architecture firm, GayMenzel, after working in New York, Basel and Hamburg. Since then, they have worked with everything from public spaces and water features to bridges and chalets, always drawing inspiration from their surroundings. "When you're designing your own home, there is a big focus on liveability and domesticity. Comfort is derived from space, light and scale," says Catherine. Their home has a warm, lived-in feel, with art, books and plants tapering up walls and spilling into one another, all set against the backdrop of the apartment's historical features. "It's not sleek and minimalist," says Götz. "The decorations might not have anything to do with one another at first sight but putting them together immediately creates new, fresh stories."

185

RESIDENCE
NEUENSCHWANDER COLONY
Gockhausen, Zürich

With few limits on space or restrictions from building regulations, Swiss modernist architect Eduard Neuenschwander allowed his imagination free rein to create a model community out of sweeping curves of concrete.

The hillside hamlet of Gockhausen, east of Zürich, is home to a planned community created by Swiss modernist architect Eduard Neuenschwander. Designed between the 1960s and late 1970s, when the area was largely rural and building restrictions were few, the ensemble of structures – which sit among verdant courtyards – is testament to the late architect's organic modernism. Neuenschwander was a fine draughtsman with a keen interest in biology, archaeology and the natural environment, and his passions found expression in his experiments with concrete and in imaginative landscaping. In its heyday, his "colony" hosted his architecture practice, his family home, a dance studio, musicians and a gallery. Today the 20-odd buildings have been mostly converted into private dwellings. Neuenschwander's residence that he shared with his second wife, Menchu (*pictured*), and son, Christian, remains. Here, the curving concrete ceiling and exposed walls show the architect's admiration for the material's versatility and resilience.

A great living space isn't just a matter of architecture – it can only come alive with the right furniture. These are the experts who can turn your residence into a home.

FURNITURE

FURNITURE
HOBEL
Zürich

Since 1959, the Hobel shop has been a fixture in Zürich's Niederdorf, a destination for those who appreciate fine craftsmanship and timeless design. About half of the boutique's contents are dedicated to Hobel's work – including tables, stools and bespoke dining tables – while the rest is a selection of high-quality brands. There are expertly crafted chairs by Horgenglarus and timeless tableware by French manufacturer Pillivuyt. Founded in 1945 as a co-operative, it still crafts furniture and fittings in a joinery workshop in Altstetten. "Here you'll find everything you need to set a dining table beautifully," says its managing director, Lutz Kögler (*pictured*). *hobel.zuerich*

FURNITURE
NEUMARKT 17
Zürich

Behind Neumarkt 17's discreet entrance is a space across multiple floors that blends quality design with unexpected finds. Founded in 1964 by architect Fritz Schwarz and his wife, Liz Schwarz, a textile designer, Neumarkt 17 is a furniture and design shop that offers tailored interior consulting to help clients craft spaces that reflect their style. The selection combines well-known brands with artisanal designs. "You just know when it works," says Andreas Schwarz, the son of Fritz and Liz, who took over in 1995. Schwarz emphasises the importance of combining industrially produced furniture with handcrafted elements, ensuring a personal touch.
neumarkt17.ch

FURNITURE
STUDIO SEBASTIAN MARBACHER
Zürich

Sebastian Marbacher has built a practice around objects that unify. "Consensus in design is always about bringing together ideas, people and disciplines," he says. Having studied design and trained in mechanical engineering, he works with wood, metal and more. For him, it is about letting the material guide the process. His studio collaborates with museums, galleries and brands, including the Museum für Gestaltung Zürich (*see page 125*), Freitag and Ishinomaki Laboratory. His approach extends beyond furniture: his take on everyday objects – such as the salt mill designed for MONOCLE – reflects a similar commitment to simplicity, function and craft.
sebastian.marbacher.com

189

FURNITURE
USM
Berne

USM specialises in modular and sustainable furniture, designed to adapt to users' needs and move easily from home to home. For more than 100 years, the Münsingen-based company has been an industry leader when it comes to the selection of materials, production and design. In Berne, the brand's showroom offers a glimpse of the endless possibilities that can be achieved with the USM system. Featuring workstations, meeting rooms and reception areas, visitors can explore the creative applications of different interior solutions and product components – an experience further enhanced by advanced modelling software guided by design specialists. *usm.com*

FURNITURE
KISSTHEDESIGN
Lausanne

When couple Yanick Fournier and Corine Stübi returned to Lausanne in 2006, they started collecting vintage designs to furnish their apartment. Four years later they found a 1927 building designed by Alphonse Laverrière, the architect behind Lausanne's train station. It was there they established their bricks-and-mortar shop. "Back then no one in Lausanne was selling mid-century vintage designs," says Fournier. Today the focus is on 20th-century pieces from the likes of Serge Mouille, Poltronova, Memphis Milano, Tacchini, Sammode, Carl Hansen & Søn, Nemo and Gubi. The couple also run the Le Salon du Design fair in Geneva. *kissthedesign.ch*

FURNITURE
VITRA
Birsfelden, Basel-Landschaft

Vitra proudly embraces its Swiss heritage from its HQ in Birsfelden. Founded in 1950 by Willi and Erika Fehlbaum, the Vitra Campus and flagship shop are a 15-minute drive from Basel in Weil am Rhein. The architectural feat houses showrooms and exhibitions that visitors can peruse for inspiration. Pieces by the likes of Charles and Ray Eames are displayed alongside the works of contemporary designers such as Konstantin Grcic, showcasing the eclectic, extensive selection that Vitra is known for. "Timeless and ever-relevant, it maintains its significance and enduring appeal across generations," says the firm's chief design officer, Christian Grosen. *vitra.com*

FURNITURE
LES BOIS
Zug

"I found it much simpler to set up my business here, particularly as I chose wood as the material," says Les Bois owner, Bianca Stoll-Gerber, who left a job as a paralegal in Zürich to open the company. Les Bois' minimalist designs are made by Swiss carpenters using sustainable methods and are known for their regulation of indoor climates and fragrances that bring crisp scents into customers' homes. Natural colour and grain variations make for characterful, individual pieces that celebrate the locally sourced wood. The Selva sideboard is Stoll-Gerber's hero product – with its subtle floating effect and delicate legs, the unit has proved enduringly popular. *shoplesbois.ch*

Whether you need to kit out a family dwelling, a chic mountain
hotel or a city-centre shop, these are the architects you'll need
to make your chosen space sing.

ARCHITECTURE
& DESIGN

MACH ARCHITEKTUR
Zürich

David Marquardt's Mach Architektur studio can be
found in the heart of Zürich, surrounded by its designs.
From apartment buildings in the Alps to the Monocle
Café in Seefeld (*see page 69*), the studio has an impressive
portfolio of projects that make use of traditional
materials and design. "Our precise Swiss heritage makes
us work in a clear, graphic and reduced artistic way," says
Marquardt. The studio favours wood, stone and glass
in its work, employing talented craftspeople and high-
quality materials to create beautiful and practical spaces.
"Great architecture needs great clients, great architects
and great craftsmen," says Marquardt.
macharch.ch

INTERIOR DESIGN
DIMANCHE
Geneva

This design hub is brimming with fresh ideas and creative solutions. Established in 2020, it offers interior-design services and a showroom of products, including objects and furniture from Carl Hansen & Søn, Hay and De Vorm. The idea is to make these spaces feel like a home – but think vibrant colours, bold shapes and unconventional materials perfect for adding personality and wit. The name ("Sunday" in French) is inspired by the day that many people spend at home and the company's aim is to dress rooms with furniture and items that bring together the contemporary, the nostalgic and the theatrical for both private and public spaces.
dimanche.swiss

ARCHITECTURE STUDIO
CAMINADA ARCHITEKTEN
Trin, Graubünden

With a creative approach connected to the landscapes and material traditions of Switzerland, Caminada Architekten has produced an impressive range of contemporary architecture using a restrained palette of wood, stone and concrete – from light-filled mountain residences to workshops, restaurants and hotels, including a bathhouse extension to the Hotel Schweizerhof in Flims (*pictured, bottom*). Helmed by Marcel Caminada, the firm is based in Trin in Graubünden. Its buildings often appear to have grown out of the forest floor – or, as in the case of the Hangar event space in Laax (*pictured, top*), to have been gently placed so as not to disturb their surroundings.
caminada-architekten.ch

You've decided where you'd like to live and what you want your new home to look like. Now it's time to get some inspiration from those who have gone before you and are already set up in Switzerland.

SUCCESS STORIES

MISAKO AKIYAMA
Zürich

Misako Akiyama had been working for 10 years at a Tokyo brewery when she first tasted a roll cake. "It was so delicious," she says. She immediately sought out a pastry-making course so she could make it at home. She eventually quit her job, moved to Tokyo and enrolled at Le Cordon Bleu culinary school. She met her German husband while training in France and the couple settled in Zürich, where Akiyama opened a pastry business (after a brief stint baking for Japanese-French café Mame). "I like to work quietly and focus, and I love pastries," says Akiyama. "My hobby became my job." She now runs a team of seven and supplies baked goods to 10 local cafés, including the Monocle Café in Seefeld (*see page 69*).

NADIA AND ANTONIO DAGO
St Moritz

On most winter evenings at the Crystal Hotel in St Moritz, music spills from the hotel's cool, dark piano bar. Married couple and locally famous duo Nadia and Antonio Dago have been playing here for some 30 years. Both are originally from Italy (Nadia from Vicenza and Antonio from Verbania) but they now spend winter in the resort town. The two met while Nadia was working as a singer at the Beau-Rivage Palace in Lausanne and pianist Antonio came to play. "We ate together every night for a week and at the end we had fallen in love," says Nadia. They married in 1996 and when not in Verbania they reside at the Crystal, where Nadia sings in 11 different languages, accompanied by her husband on piano.

HOTELIER
RUTH KRAMER
Vals, Graubünden

Ruth Kramer first visited Vals in 1999 and it took a single breath of Alpine air to persuade her to move there. "My inner Heidi was awoken," she says. "This was where I wanted home to be." Kramer had a successful career as a fashion designer working with H&M and Inditex in Denmark but shortly after she and her late husband bought an old house on the riverfront that they transformed into Brücke 49 (*see page 27*), followed by Brücke Herberge Apartments. Both blend Scandinavian design with Swiss straightforwardness. Kramer works with local craftspeople with a philosophy that emphasises timelessness and authenticity. "My places should aim to honour the beauty and value of nature," she says.

JOHANNA VAN DER DRIFT AND DAAN VAN LUIJN
Berne

"What's unique about working in Switzerland is the beauty of the country," says Heigs' founder, Johanna van der Drift, who moved there 20 years ago with her family and now splits her time between Berne (where the brand's HQ is located) and Paris (the bags are produced in France). In 2022 she was joined by business partner Daan van Luijn (*pictured, on left, with Van der Drift*), who's based in New York and has spent time in the Swiss Alps. "Our mission is to shine a light on handmade craftsmanship in a world where this artistry is becoming increasingly rare," he says. Their advice to successfully set up shop is to embrace the country's sense of quality and simplicity. "Get to know the rhythm of Swiss life," says Van der Drift.

HANNA AND JOHAN OLZON ÅKERSTRÖM
Zürich

Hanna Olzon Åkerström and her husband, Johan, both Swedish expats, met in Zürich in 2008. Soon after, the architect and product engineer had the idea of making soap from natural ingredients. "As young parents, we studied the ingredients of common washing lotions and then stood in our kitchen to make soap containing fewer chemicals," says Hanna. Their first shop, Soeder, opened in 2013 and collaborations with Swiss International Air Lines, VitraHaus (*see page 191*) and the Cervo Mountain Resort in Zermatt (*see page 19*) furthered its success. In 2023, for the brand's 10th anniversary, production was moved to a former railway-repair facility in Zürich, which Hanna designed.

PART 03

ADDRESS BOOK

Take a tour of the best in Swiss hospitality, design,
culture and shopping – plus the attractions and
activities not to be missed.

ZÜRICH

Switzerland's largest and busiest city is the powerhouse of the modern Swiss nation. Along with the eponymous canton that surrounds it, Zürich is truly a global city and a centre for culture, food and tourism, as well as being a hub for transport, banking and business.

STAY

THE DOLDER GRAND
Hottingen
A convenient combination of urban access and restorative vistas, offering 175 luxurious rooms and suites, numerous restaurants and one of the largest spas in Switzerland.
thedoldergrand.com

HOTEL EUROPE
Seefeld
On the doorstep of the Opera House, Hotel Europe is a charming boutique stay with brightly styled rooms and a penchant for intricate antiquities.
europehotel.ch

SIGNAU HOUSE
Riesbach
This small hotel was built in 1912 as a two-storey aristocratic mansion and renovated in 2018 to create a discreet location removed from the city's bustle.
signauhouse.com

MANDARIN ORIENTAL SAVOY
Altstadt
This premium bolthole boasts 80 rooms, including the city's 36 largest suites. All have been decked out by Paris-based Tristan Auer with bespoke furnishings, curated artwork and a subtle colour palette.
mandarinoriental.com

THE HOME
Enge
Defined by its artistic flair and playful spirit, The Home hotel is a quirky, Dadaist urban bolthole.
thehomehotel.ch

STORCHEN
Altstadt
Occupying a spot on the Limmat for over six centuries, Storchen is a bastion of Swiss opulence.
storchen.ch

Classic cuisine at Kronenhalle

WIDDER
Altstadt
Spanning nine medieval townhouses, the 49 rooms and suites and four luxury residences are a deft blend of traditional features and modern design elements.
widderhotel.com

ALEX LAKE
Thalwil (Zürich, canton)
A lakeside haven for those craving solace, this hotel offers comfort and luxury in all its forms, from well-equipped, deluxe studios to plush, elegant penthouses.
alexlakezurich.com

BAUR AU LAC
Altstadt
Now in the hands of the seventh generation of owners, this family-run hotel is imbued with a sense of comfort and familiarity.
bauraulac.ch

EAT & DRINK

JUCKER FARM
Seegräben (Zürich, canton)
This agricultural oasis has gardens for foraging, an orchard and views of the rolling hills and Lake Pfäffikon. Re-engage with the rustic in this verdant haven.
juckerfarm.ch

H SCHWARZENBACH
Altstadt
The Schwarzenbach family have developed a reputation for quality sweet treats and coffee thanks to their esteemed espresso bar, delicatessen and chocolate shop.
schwarzenbach.ch

GELATI
Langstrasse
Offering 30 different varieties of ice cream and sorbet, this light, airy space is a divine spot in which to enjoy some handmade Italian-style scoops.
gelati1998.ch

OSSO
Langstrasse
This buzzy restaurant found in Zürich's popular Langstrasse neighbourhood highlights Swiss cuisine, while also embracing new and exciting dishes.
ossozuerich.ch

TSUGI
Langstrasse
Tsugi combines Japan's umami flavours with ancient leavening techniques, creating crowd-pleasers such as the salty seaweed croissant.
tsugi.ch

OXEN
Küsnacht
Founded by MONOCLE chairman and editorial director Tyler Brûlé and associates, this modern kitchen serves reimagined dishes of hearty classics.
oxen.ch

SAMIGO AMUSEMENT
Enge
In a uniquely Swiss style, Samigo offers gastronomy and outdoor sports in a colourful way.
samigo.ch

KRONENHALLE
Altstadt
Famed for its impeccable service and delectable takes on French and Swiss classics, this restaurant has perfected understated hospitality.
kronenhalle.com

SCHNUPF
Aussersihl
This restaurant-cum-bar serves quality dishes and drinks in its dimly-lit dining room on cosy nights and a shaded garden on sunny days.
schnupf.bar

KUNSTHAUS BAR
Altstadt
A prized place for encounters between art and cuisine, this bar is a prime location for a stop-off while visiting the Kunsthaus Zürich.
kunsthausbar.ch

CHARLATAN RESTODISCO
Aussersihl
Established in 2022 and influenced by the dazzling parties of past eras, this is a rare establishment where disco balls and haute cuisine meet.
restodisco.ch

CHOUPETTE
Enge
This colourful, modern brasserie offers 40 outdoor seats for a sundowner – perhaps after a swim in the nearby Seebad Enge.
choupette.zuerich

LA STANZA
Enge
Politicians and financiers frequent La Stanza for its coffee, its choice of print newspapers and chilled playlists.
lastanza.ch

IM VIADUKT
Gewerbeschule
Under 36 arches there is a mix of independent boutiques, studios, art galleries and culinary hotspots.
im-viadukt.ch

Gül's inviting garden

COLLECTIVE BAKERY
Escher Wyss
A team of passionate bakers prepares goodies that blend multiple culinary traditions. The most popular product remains a famously flaky variation of a hand-rolled French croissant.
collectivebakery.ch

MONOCLE CAFÉ
Seefeld
Since opening in 2018 the Monocle Café has become the top address to grab a coffee and pick up the latest issue of the magazine.
Dufourstrasse 90

NUDE
Wipkingen
With its yellow tables, floor-to-ceiling windows and steady hum of chatter, this café is a reliable location for a good coffee with friends.
nude-zurich.com

CONFISERIE SPRÜNGLI
Altstadt
Founded in 1836, Confiserie Sprüngli sets the benchmark with its divine buttery pralines and Grand Cru varieties.
spruengli.ch

GÜL
Langstrasse
As Zürich's food scene continues to transform into a richly layered, multicultural tapestry, Gül's spiced-up take on traditional Turkish dishes stands out as a colourful addition.
guel.ch

BRASSERIE SÜD
Altstadt
Open for an early morning breakfast or a late-night dinner, Brasserie Süd offers sophisticated cuisine throughout the day, putting a creative spin on traditional dishes.
brasserie-sued.ch

BAR LUPO
Sihlfeld
A trendy, central location that serves hearty pasta dishes alongside fashionable, experimental cocktails and elegant wines.
lupo.bar

ORA BAR
Altstadt
In the hands of esteemed cocktail artist Marco Colelli and emerging chef Ken Rojas, this bar offers drinks and small plates in an intimate setting.
ora-bar.ch

BARRANCO
Hard
Inspired by the flavourful cuisine of the Barranco district in Peru, this namesake restaurant showcases a vibrant mix of dishes that are best enjoyed when shared.
barranco.ch

HOI KOI
Sihlfeld
Hoi Koi's ever-changing seasonal menu is the creation of chef Zhou Qinhan, who prepares Japanese dishes with flair and panache.
hoikoi.ch

MIRÓ
Langstrasse
A café and roastery producing delicious speciality coffee, owned by brothers Daniel and David Sanchez.
mirocoffee.co

SHOP

QWSTION
Escher Wyss
Born out of a mission to revolutionise the textile industry, Zürich-based label Qwstion offers bags made from plants instead of plastic.
qwstion.com

TRUNK
Seefeld
Brushing shoulders with our very own Monocle Café, the smart menswear products from both in-house designs and international offerings allow customers to build a wardrobe with ease.
trunkclothiers.com

ENSOIE
Altstadt
This five-storey flagship housed in a 14th-century building has the biggest range of the brand's homeware as well as cheery dresses, coats and handwoven scarves.
ensoie.com

OPIA
Langstrasse
Having opened in 2008, this multibrand boutique was inspired by Claudia Desax's time in Bangkok.
opia.ch

JIM GERBER
Altstadt
Head to vintage watch specialist Jim Gerber to get your hands on a time-tested Rolex or Patek Philippe.
jimgerber.com

A relaxed experience at Trunk

THE APARTMENT STORE
Altstadt
This multi-brand shop is home to a number of Swiss and international labels, from Kiner ceramics to contemporary womenswear brand Claudia Bertini.
theapartmentstore.ch

BALLY
Altstadt
Bally began in 1851 as a family business known for inventive shoe-making. The brand has since become a fully-fledged fashion label offering cheeky but understated clothes.
bally.com

SÜSKIND
Altstadt
The cosy shop is in a 300-year-old building featuring wooden shelves stocked with big names and lesser-known fragrance brands.
sueskind.ch

FABRIKAT
Langstrasse
The homeware, stationery and craft tools emporium carries a timeless selection of goods with a versatile inventory that solves everyday predicaments with practical solutions.
fabrikat.ch

HIOO
Langstrasse
An overarching store containing three distinct shops, each offering different types of furniture from vintage to modern and re-editions, plus a warehouse store full of one-offs and other rarities.
h100.ch

MAKING THINGS
Langstrasse
This bright three-room shop is found in the city's colourful Langstrasse neighbourhood and offers a selection of clothing, jewellery and accessories.
makingthings.ch

MARTIN GROSSENBACHER BLUMEN
Seefeld
Since 1997, Martin Grossenbacher and his dedicated team of florists have been providing the highest quality flowers in Seefeld.
martingrossenbacher.ch

NEUMARKT 17
Altstadt
Neumarkt 17 offers tailored interior consulting to help clients craft spaces that reflect their style, balancing mainstream pieces with unique finds.
neumarkt17.ch

LIMITED STOCK
Altstadt
This chamber of curiosity does what it says on the tin: here, stock is limited with a portfolio of creative brands produced in small batches.
limited-stock.com

ZERO ZERO RARE GROOVE
Aussersihl
Known for its eclectic mix of records – new and secondhand, international and local, rare and classical – Zero Zero Rare Groove has something to suit everyone.
Bäckerstrasse 54

PARADIS COLLECTIONS
Altstadt
This womenswear boutique offers high-quality, timeless clothing, as well as a bespoke service designed to fulfil personal requests ahead of special occasions.
paradiscollections.ch

HOBEL
Altstadt
Furniture maker and vendor Hobel has had a store in Zurich since 1959. It still operates a joinery workshop in the city's Altstetten district, where it creates its own products and fashions bespoke pieces.
hobel.zuerich

HOCHPARTERRE BÜCHER
Langstrasse
Switzerland's only bookshop dedicated to architecture stocks over 3,000 titles on the subject.
hochparterre-buecher.ch

VICTORINOX
Altstadt
With precision and a commitment to heritage, Victorinox is the pioneer of the original Swiss Army Knife.
victorinox.com

NEVER STOP READING
Altstadt
Teeming with insightful books on architecture, photography, art and design, Never Stop Reading boasts an eclectic mix of in-house and international works across a variety of languages.
neverstopreading.com

Modernism at Pavillon Le Corbusier

DO

MUSEUM FÜR GESTALTUNG ZÜRICH
Escher Wyss
With more than half a million objects, this impressive museum is home to the country's largest design collection.
museum-gestaltung.ch

PAVILLON LE CORBUSIER
Seefeld
It is fitting that Le Corbusier's swansong is located in the country of his birth. The space is dedicated to the work of the modernist master.
pavillon-le-corbusier.ch

EDITION VFO
Escher Wyss
A gallery, publisher and arts institute at the Löwenbräukunst-Areal centre focused on printmaking.
edition-vfo.ch

MOODS
Escher Wyss
This former shipbuilding hall is now one of Europe's leading clubs to soak up jazz, soul, funk and blues.
moods.ch

KUNSTHAUS ZÜRICH
Altstadt
Including both public and privately owned works, this respected museum has one of the largest art collections in Switzerland.
kunsthaus.ch

KUNST MUSEUM WINTERTHUR
Winterthur (Zürich, canton)
A wide-ranging selection of art displayed across three buildings set in verdant parks in Switzerland's former industrial heartland.
kmw.ch

BERNHEIM
Altstadt
To celebrate emerging talent, the exhibitions at Bernheim gallery connect lesser-known artists with existing art traditions.
bernheimgallery.com

LARKIN ERDMANN
Altstadt
A distinctive presence in the contemporary art world, the gallery predominantly focuses on post-war artists, from the 1940-1960 period.
larkinerdmann.com

CABARET VOLTAIRE
Altstadt
At Cabaret Voltaire, an eccentric café-cum-cabaret, the anti-establishment art movement known as Dadaism is actively explored.
cabaretvoltaire.ch

GENEVA & WEST

Geneva is Switzerland's second-largest city and the largest in the French-speaking western part of the country. It is a truly global hub and hosts the headquarters for many international bodies, including the Red Cross, Cern, the World Trade Organisation and numerous UN agencies.

STAY

THE WOODWARD
Pâquis
The 26-suite hotel on the shore of Lake Geneva is famed for its views of Mont Blanc and proximity to the glittering water of the Plage des Pâquis outdoor pool.
aubergeresorts.com

LA RÉSERVE GENÈVE
Bellevue (Geneva, canton)
Set in ten acres of landscaped greenery overlooking the lake, this tranquil oasis exudes relaxation, taking its inspiration from the refined style of African lodges.
lareserve-geneve.com

HÔTEL LES ARMURES
Cité-Centre
Perfectly situated at the foot of the beautiful Saint-Pierre cathedral, Les Armures is a warmly decorated affair with an ambient restaurant designed in the typical well-measured Swiss manner.
lesarmures.ch

HÔTEL-RESTAURANT DU PARC DES EAUX-VIVES
Eaux-Vives
A stunning terrace punctuates this immense property in one of central Geneva's quaintest parks. If you're after the perfect cocktail of cosiness and luxury, check yourself in here.
parcdeseauxvives.ch

FOUR SEASONS HÔTEL DES BERGUES
Saint-Gervais
With rooms designed by the illustrious Pierre-Yves Rochon, a serene rooftop spa and a gourmet Michelin-starred restaurant, Geneva's oldest luxury hotel has long been a favourite among sophisticated travellers.
fourseasons.com

Good times in the sun at Bleu Nuit

EAT & DRINK

RESTAURANT ROBERTO
Cité-Centre
Generations of Genevans have returned to Roberto since its opening in 1945 – a testament to the restaurant's dedication to creating proper Italian fare.
restaurantroberto.ch

FISKEBAR
Pâquis
With a regularly changing menu that is revised every two months, Fiskebar bridges cultures with its inspired flavour combinations and range of biodynamic wines.
fiskebar.ch

BOMBAR
Plainpalais
There's something festive about Bombar's approach to mealtimes. European-style small plates and aromatic wines are served until 22.30 – almost unheard of in Geneva.
bombar.ch

NINO
Plainpalais
A neighbourhood bottle shop specialising in biodynamic wine, microbrews and local cider.
ninocave.com

HALLE DE RIVE
Cité-Centre
A culinary metropolis set back from a busy street, Halle de Rive showcases some of the best Geneva has to offer.
halle-de-rive.ch

BLEU NUIT
Plainpalais
At Bleu Nuit, diners perch at the long steel bar for a plate of charcuterie, a bowl of cockles or a fine selection of cheeses.
Rue du Vieux-Billard 4

CAFÉ DE LA PAIX
Plainpalais
This lively, light-filled restaurant is versatile and relaxed. In the evenings it transforms into a dimly lit, intimate bistro, perfect for a late-night aperitif.
cafe-delapaix.ch

MARIUS
Plainpalais
Situated in a century-old former *boucherie* (butcher's shop), Marius is something between a Basque *pintxo* bar and a Japanese *izakaya*.
Place des Augustins 9

LAMIETTE
Cité-Centre
Unlike Geneva's traditional bakeries, Lamiette's interior feels unstuffy and modern. But it's the viennoiserie which take centre stage.
Rue de Saint-Léger 5

AUER
Cité-Centre
This family-run independent chocolatier founded in 1939 manufactures more than 50 types of luxury chocolate.
chocolat-auer.ch

LE LYRIQUE
Plainpalais
Brimming with character, Geneva's oldest restaurant-brasserie boasts a spacious terrace, an ornate Second Empire ceiling and grand pillars, making for an unparalleled fine dining experience.
cafe-lyrique.ch

LA MAISON DU FROMAGE STERCHI
Neuchâtel (Neuchâtel, canton)
Nurtured through generations, La Maison du Fromage Sterchi is a family-owned fromagerie that has cultivated its passion for cheese since its founding in 1928.
sterchi-fromages.ch

SHOP

MONSIEUR ALAIN
Plainpalais
With a collection of some of the most prominent names in menswear on offer, you'll undoubtedly find your new favourite threads.
monsieuralain.ch

BONGÉNIE GENÈVE
Cité-Centre
As well as an impressive seven levels worth of high-end fashion, a beauty salon, perfumery, workshop and various dining options can be found in this luxury department store.
stores.bongenie.ch

THE L STORE
Saint-Gervais
The L Store showcases the best of local Swiss fashion, offering clothing, jewellery and accessories designed by Mademoiselle L and invited guests.
thelstore.ch

LES AMBASSADEURS
Cité-Centre
Since 1964, this Swiss institution has curated timepieces from the world's most prestigious maisons.
lesambassadeurs.ch

POPPY
Plainpalais
For a beautiful bouquet of pigmented colours and ambrosial scents, be sure to swing by this expert florist.
poppyshop.ch

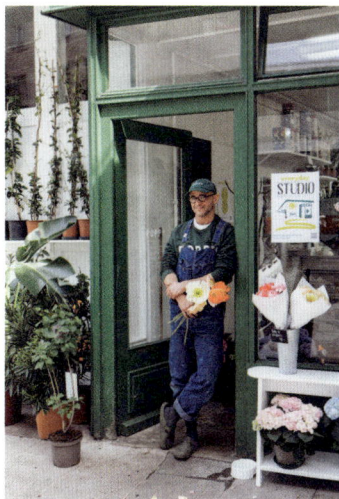

Poppy will brighten up your day

HORLOGERIE DESBIOLLES
Cité-Centre
A quietly revered atelier founded in 1986, this charming, old-world workshop not only restores timepieces but also offers a selection of vintage treasures.
artisanhorloger.ch

PARADIGME
Eaux-Vives
Carrying the works of well-known designers including Paraboot, A Kind of Guise and Maison Fabre, Paradigme presents a comprehensive wardrobe of high-quality clothing and accessories.
boutiqueparadigme.com

LES ENFANTS TERRIBLES
Plainpalais
In this interior design showroom, visitors will find a thoughtful mix of vintage and modern pieces selected to help them realise beautiful spaces.
les-enfants-terribles.ch

DO

CERN SCIENCE GATEWAY
Meyrin (Geneva, canton)
A dynamic hub for exploration, innovation and discovery, the Cern Science Gateway is a space for visitors to engage with science up close.
visit.cern

MUSÉE D'ART ET D'HISTOIRE
Cité-Centre
The museum's encyclopaedic collection includes some 650,000 objects, ranging from historic portrait miniatures and local archaeological finds to rare books and fine art.
mahmah.ch

WILDE
Plainpalais
The gallery is a cornucopia of contemporary art, showcasing a diverse collection of works across two floors of exhibition spaces.
wildegallery.ch

PATEK PHILIPPE MUSEUM
Plainpalais
Here you'll find an impressive display of creations by the brand's most vaunted watchmakers who, along with Rolex and many other watch brands, still call the city home.
patek.com

BAINS DES PÂQUIS
Pâquis
Fancy a swim? These open-water baths in the heart of the city are open every day. There are also sauna facilities and food available – readily enjoyed by locals and tourists alike.
aubp.ch

GENEVA & WEST

THE ADDRESS BOOK

CENTRAL

The central area of Switzerland is based around the Alpine cantons that came together in the 13th century to form the Old Swiss Confederacy, the precursor of the modern nation. The landscape is dominated by lakes and mountains, making tourism very important to the region.

STAY

HÔTEL BEAU SÉJOUR
Lucerne
A secret haven in one of Switzerland's tourist hotspots, the 1875 building features intricate parquet floors, three-metre-high ceilings and 1970s-style vintage tiled bathrooms.
beausejourlucerne.ch

PARK HOTEL VITZNAU
Vitznau
This veritable jewel of a hotel overlooks Lake Lucerne and its glimmering waters, offering a painterly view no matter the season. Two fine-dining restaurants and a hydrotherapy pool contribute to the hotel's health and wellness agenda.
parkhotel-vitznau.ch

ART DECO HOTEL MONTANA
Lucerne
If the art deco movement stirs you, you'll feel at home in this elaborate and beautifully composed hotel close to Lake Lucerne.
hotel-montana.ch

EAT & DRINK

BRASSERIE KONRAD
Engelberg (Obwalden)
Inspired by the informal and lively atmosphere of a classic brasserie, Brasserie Konrad serves the best of Swiss comfort food – perfect after a long day on the slopes.
skilodgeengelberg.com

BRASSERIE BODU
Lucerne
This self-proclaimed *französische* (French) brasserie feels more like a Parisian bistro than a Swiss *stübli*.
brasseriebodu.ch

MILL'FEUILLE
Lucerne
Indulge in delicious sweet treats and savoury bites here in the sunlit glass conservatory or on the riverfront.
millfeuille.ch

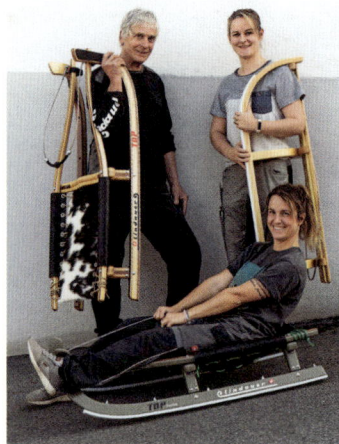
It's all downhill at Lindauer

CATTANI RESTAURANT
Engelberg (Obwalden)
This bright, high-ceilinged spot blends an elegant atmosphere with the best of French-Swiss cuisine. The stunning Alpine views on offer don't go amiss, either.
kempinski.com

MAGDALENA BÄCKEREI
Rickenbach (Schwyz)
In the space beneath the namesake restaurant, Magdalena Bäckerei spoils its customers with fresh baguettes, fluffy croissants, cinnamon knots, pains au chocolat and Danish pastries.
restaurant-magdalena.ch

SHOP

ATELIER TREGER
Lucerne
Atelier Treger was Switzerland's first boutique dedicated to braces. Since then, the collection has diversified to include bow ties and pocket squares, as well as bespoke suits and men's and womenswear.
treger.ch

STÖCKLI
Malters (Lucerne)
Applauded for meticulous attention to detail, Stöckli produce around 75,000 pairs of skis every year and remain committed to manufacturing their products by hand.
stoeckli.ch

MUOSER
Schattdorf (Uri)
This furniture retailer hosts some of the best Scandi and Nordic designers on the market. With a range spanning asymmetric sofas to sculptural lighting and brands like Muuto and &Tradition, if it's good design you're after, you're in safe hands.
muoser.ch

LINDAUER
Schwyz (Schwyz)
In this sporty region of the Swiss Alps, the name Lindauer is synonymous with the finest (and fastest) sledges on the slopes.
lindauerschlitten.ch

DO

BIOSPHÄRE ENTLEBUCH
Entlebuch (Lucerne)
This Unesco-protected zone is Switzerland's largest area of moorland, with weaving, hilly paths to explore and the chance to observe all kinds of flora and fauna. Verdant views await.
biosphaere.ch

TICINO

Switzerland's southernmost canton is home to almost half of the country's Italian-speakers and is a unique combination of Italian and Swiss influences. Ticino is linked to the rest of the nation via the Gotthard Base Tunnel – the longest rail tunnel in the world.

STAY

VILLA CASTAGNOLA
Lugano
A luxurious sanctuary for aristocrats, artists and intellectuals, the 71 rooms and suites all offer a view of the lake and the subtropical park.
villacastagnola.com

CASA SISU
Tesserete
Hotelier Ramona Casale learned her hospitality lessons in Campania, southern Italy and created a cosy six-key guesthouse which looks out onto the residence's garden.
casa-sisu.ch

VILLA PINETA
Fusio
A renovated Swiss chalet-style villa, this historic nine-key property has a library, film nights and concert nights in the music hall.
villapineta.ch

EAT & DRINK

GROTTINO TICINESE
Bellinzona
Low-key, unpretentious Italian fare including *vitello tonnato* and cold cuts from Graübunden feature on the menu at this charming restaurant that occupies a building constructed in 1929.
grottinoticinesebellinzona.ch

TRANI
Lugano
Lugano's restaurants tend to err on the traditional side but this osteria is a distinctly Mediterranean affair. There's also an extensive wine list showcasing Swiss, Italian and French appellations.
trani.ch

View at LAC Lugano Arte e Cultura

ACQUA E FARINA
Lugano
Meaning water and flour, simply put this is undiluted Neapolitan pizza topped with buffalo mozzarella, Campano tomatoes and plenty of fresh basil leaves.
acqua-farina.ch

RISTORANTE ALLA CANTINA
Tegna
Find rustic Sicilian cuisine here, including crunchy cannoli filled with creamy ricotta and generous portions of pasta alla norma.
ristorantealllacantina.com

SHOP

AVART
Lugano
Spanning two beautifully designed retail spaces, Avart's shelves are expertly stocked with clothing and accessories, serving as living proof that the brick-and-mortar shopping experience can't be replicated online.
avart.ch

LAC SHOP
Lugano
The LAC cultural centre's well-stocked bookstore has a focus on art, photography, fashion, design and architecture.
lacshop.ch

PRESTIGE BOUTIQUE
Lugano
Well-heeled locals head here to find Tod's leather loafers, cross-body bags by Ganni and tailored jackets by Vince.
prestigeboutique.ch

DO

LAC LUGANO ARTE E CULTURA
Lugano
This angular arts centre stands over Lake Lugano and contains all manner of interdisciplinary media: you'll get your culture fix here.
luganolac.ch

LA FABBRICA
Losone
Once the Mornaghini Furniture Factory, today the converted premises house music and dance classes, a bakery, artist studios and even a beer tavern.
lafabbrica.ch

CENTRAL & TICINO

THE ADDRESS BOOK

SOUTHWEST

The southwestern area of Switzerland includes glamorous Alpine resorts such as Zermatt and Verbier, smaller rural communities and larger lakeside centres including Lausanne and Montreux. The proximity to France gives the areas close to the border a distinct Gallic influence and feel.

STAY

SIX SENSES
Crans Montana (Valais)
This ski-in, ski-out retreat swaps old-fashioned chalet style for bold architecture, pairing angular lines with warm, organic materials.
sixsenses.com

MICHELHAUS
Ernen (Valais)
Welcoming visitors to the 800-year-old mountain town of Ernen with a stone hearth and a medley of antiques, this two-apartment retreat is the triumph of Reto Holzer.
michelhaus.ch

GRAND HOTEL ZERMATTERHOF
Zermatt
Popular among celebrities, royalty, and hikers, this hotel offers an inherently Swiss stay enhanced by traditional, Michelin-starred dining.
zermatterhof.ch

THE OMNIA
Zermatt
A luxurious modern interpretation of a classic mountain lodge, nestled in the shadow of the Matterhorn.
the-omnia.com

LE CHALET LION ROUGE
Rougemont (Vaud)
This newly renovated 300-year-old farmhouse promises a moment of peace in nature.
84rooms.com

EXPERIMENTAL CHALET
Verbier
This outpost of the Experimental Group is highly styled and draws an equally canny crowd to its 39 rooms.
experimentalchalet.com

CERVO
Zermatt
With 54 rooms and suites located in wooden peaked-roof chalets, Cervo has a chic take on Alpine luxury.
cervo.swiss

Ski in, eat at Six Senses, then ski out

BEAU-RIVAGE PALACE
Lausanne
The epitome of quintessential luxury, this 168-key hotel boasts idyllic mountain views, elegant dining spots and an impressive grand ballroom.
brp.ch

EAT & DRINK

CHEZ DANY
Verbier
Chez Dany is tucked away from the crowded piste restaurants. On the menu is Swiss fare which doesn't take itself too seriously and hearty dishes from beyond Swiss borders.
chezdany.ch

LAITERIE DE VERBIER
Verbier
This family-run establishment proudly provides an array of fresh, creamy cheeses, milks and yoghurts, as well as local artisanal products, including juices, jams and saucisson.
laiterie-verbier.ch

CABANE MONT FORT
Verbier
Poised at 2,457 metres, this high-altitude restaurant is delightfully exclusive. A rustic refuge built in 1925, the magnificent mountainous panoramas and hearty Swiss dishes are unparalleled.
cabanemontfort.com

L'ÉCURIE
Verbier
The restaurant serves refined dishes in the heart of Verbier. While the terrace calls for long summer lunches, the caveau is the place to dine while tasting their local and international wine selection.
restaurantecurie.ch

LA GRAPPE D'OR
Lausanne
With a flavourful menu that evolves with the seasons, the chefs at La Grappe d'Or take an authentic and refined approach to Italian cuisine.
la-grappe.ch

BUVETTE DE JAMAN
Montreux (Vaud)
In the mountains above Lake Geneva, this charming hut serves Swiss delights. Its rustic atmosphere and culinary excellence guarantees a nourishing stop in nature.
Station, Col de Jaman, 1824

MONTREUX JAZZ CAFÉ
Montreux (Vaud)
At this venue you can enjoy fine cuisine and a signature cocktail in the company of some soothing melodies and a treasure trove of music memorabilia.
montreuxjazzcafe.com

ST JODERN KELLEREI
Visperterminen (Valais)
Switzerland's most spectacular vineyard climbs steeply to a height of 1,150 metres and is famous for wines vinified with the heida grape.
jodernkellerei.ch

MARCHÉ DE LA VIEILLE VILLE DE SION
Sion (Valais)
Framed by two iconic hills – one topped with a fortified basilica and the other with a medieval castle – the town of Sion is a charming backdrop for this weekly fresh-produce market.
mvvsion.ch

RESTAURANT LA FROMAGERIE
Leysin (Vaud)
From *rösti* and *raclettes* to croûtes and fondue, visitors frequent this rustic 17th-century chalet for traditional Swiss dishes, many of which contain homemade cheese.
lafromagerie-leysin.com

COFFEE PAGE
Lausanne
2019 saw the establishment of Lausanne's first café-library, where visitors can enjoy speciality coffee roasted in Tübingen.
coffee-page.com

SHOP

DURIG
Lausanne
Durig is one of the top chocolatiers in Lausanne. With two venues in the city, it's a must-visit for any cocoa connoisseur.
durig.ch

MUSIC SOUNDS BETTER WITH BOOKS
Lausanne
A book and record store championing visual art and culture publications, hard-to-find references and vintage indie magazines.
msbwb.ch

TEMPO
Lausanne
Tempo provides a selection of tasteful design objects from across the world. From furniture to luxurious leather goods, their products embrace their ethos of slow living.
tempodesignstore.com

Marché de la Vieille Ville de Sion

KISSTHEDESIGN
Lausanne
Kissthedesign is akin to a collector's apartment. Here you'll find rare, high-end vintage design items, along with furniture and lighting discovered at design fairs and in interior magazines.
kissthedesign.ch

DO

PLATEFORME 10
Lausanne
On the site of former railway locomotive repair depot, Lausanne's Plateforme 10 arts district combines design, art and photography.
plateforme10.ch

MUSÉE ATELIER AUDEMARS PIGUET
Le Brassus (Vaud)
The museum occupies the site where the founders originally set up their workshop. Today, it houses some 300 timepieces, alongside ateliers where skilled artisans continue to craft pieces by hand.
museeatelier.audemarspiguet.com

FONDATION OPALE
Lens (Valais)
A highly recommended après-ski alternative, the exhibitions at Foundation Opale aim to help indigenous Australian art reach a wider audience.
fondationopale.ch

CAPITOLE
Lausanne
Capitole, Switzerland's largest heritage movie theatre, offers a nostalgic cinema experience redolent of the golden age of film.
cinematheque.ch

GALERIE GRANDE FONTAINE
Sion (Valais)
Among small shops on cobbled streets, the idyllic town of Sion also harbours this gallery, showcasing artistic talents from the canton of Valais and beyond.
grandefontaine.com

L'APPARTEMENT
Vevey (Vaud)
From the outside, this space looks like a train station. But a trip to the second floor reveals a trove of contemporary digital media.
images.ch

EAST

Graubünden canton is dominated by the Alps, with much of the economy revolving around Alpine tourism and winter sports. It is also the home of Romansh, a derivative of Roman Latin that survived in the mountain valleys and is now one of the four official Swiss languages.

STAY

SUVRETTA HOUSE
St Moritz
Offering unparalleled hospitality and exclusive access to the Corviglia ski area, this luxury resort is ideal for both ski enthusiasts and those seeking uninterrupted relaxation.
suvrettahouse.ch

BADRUTT'S PALACE
St Moritz
Adorned with antique furniture, this classic hotel's elegant rooms and suites offer magnificent views of the nearby lake and village centre.
badruttspalace.com

PIZ LINARD
Lavin (Graubünden)
A hotel with 20 very different rooms, the neoclassical Piz Linard has enchanted guests since 1871.
ottomesi.ch

PONTISELLA
Stampa (Graubünden)
Alongside the four guest rooms named after aromatic herbs, the highlight here is breakfast, which is prepared using fresh local produce.
pontisella-stampa.ch

ALPENGOLD HOTEL
Davos
The oval-shaped building known as the "golden egg" has a latticework façade divided by the balconies of its 216 rooms and suites.
alpengoldhotel.com

CHESA GRISCHUNA
Klosters (Graubünden)
Once a dilapidated inn and now a stunning Bündner Haus, Hans Guler first opened the doors here in 1938.
chesagrischuna.ch

CASA CAMINADA
Fürstenau (Graubünden)
Ten simple yet elegant rooms with mountain views, as well as a relaxed restaurant and a bakery.
casacaminada.com

Suvretta House's winter wonderland

TSCHUGGEN GRAND HOTEL
Arosa (Graubünden)
Defined by futuristic architecture and classic but playful interiors, the 128 rooms and suites are tailored for comfort, with deep armchairs and panoramic mountain views.
tschuggencollection.ch

BRÜCKE 49
Vals (Graubünden)
This chic Swiss accommodation at the gateway to the Tomül Pass in the Alpine village of Vals consists of a pair of thoughtfully renovated heritage buildings.
brucke49.ch

KURHAUS BERGÜN
Bergün (Graubünden)
A Jugendstil gem on the Albula Pass, the Kurhaus Bergün showcases its covetable period aspects. Sparingly decorated rooms highlight the architectural details.
kurhausberguen.ch

VILLA FLOR
S-chanf (Graubünden)
In 2009, the 1904 classicist patrician house was restored, transforming the seven rooms using family heirlooms, flea-market finds, vintage lamps and mid-century classics.
villaflor.ch

BERGHUUS RADONS
Radons (Graubünden)
A beautifully reimagined wooden lodge, Berghuus Radons has become more than a destination; for many, it is a cherished stopover on the way to St Moritz.
berghuus.ch

EAT & DRINK

ALTER TORKEL
Jenins (Graubünden)
This simple building with a terracotta-tiled roof holds a lofty position over the Bündner Herrschaft wine region and the menu matches exquisite dishes with exclusively local wine.
alter-torkel.ch

BELMONT
St Moritz
This is the perfect spot to catch up with a friend – grab a coffee in the day and stay for the gradual transformation into an ambient late-night bar.
belmontstmoritz.com

KULM COUNTRY CLUB
St Moritz
The menu at Kulm Country Club showcases local produce, with a mixture of inspired international dishes and Engadine specialities.
kulm.com

HANSELMANN
St Moritz
With a history dating back to 1894, Hanselmann cakes and treats are freshly made daily.
hanselmann.ch

GARDE-MANGER
Ardez (Graubünden)
Run by a brother-sister duo, this pastry and gourmet shop in the village of Ardez serves dishes that reflect the region's variety.
garde-manger.ch

OBRECHT WEINGUT
Jenins (Graubünden)
Assisted by a helpful local microclimate, this visionary winery uses holistic methods to promote soil health in its vineyards, with much-lauded results.
obrecht.ch

RESTAURANT BERGFÜHRER
Sertig Dörfli (Graubünden)
This historic house is the domain of chef Nina Eyer, who serves modern Swiss food at an elevated level.
sertigtal.ch

LANGOSTERIA
St Moritz
A partially open kitchen on the slopes of the Corviglia, this location is a unique culinary experience.
langosteria.com

SHOP

CASHMERE HOUSE LAMM
St Moritz
This fourth-generation cashmere company has one of the largest collections of cashmere products in the world.
cashmerelamm.ch

PESKO
Lenzerheide (Graubünden)
Established in 1911, Pesko boasts an impressive collection of skiwear and sports equipment.
pesko.ch

ROOM
Klosters (Graubünden)
Room offers a blend of Swiss heritage and international brands in fashion, art and interior design.
Bahnhofstrasse 13

GIOVANOLI SPORT & MODA
Sils Maria
The third generation of Giovanolis supplies outerwear, ski equipment and high-quality fashion brands.
giovanoli-sils.ch

The artist and his work at Atelier Bolt

EBNETER & BIEL
St Moritz
Now in its fourth generation, this traditional family-run business offers hand-embroidered linens embellished with intricate hand-drawn motifs.
ebneter-biel.ch

SUPER MOUNTAIN MARKET
St Moritz
Looking to fill a gap in the Engadine's creative scene, this multidisciplinary space offers the right combination of culture, artisanship, design and cuisine.
superstmoritz.com

TESSANDA
Santa Maria Val Müstair (Graubünden)
Tessanda is one of the country's last remaining weaving mills. Its textiles focus on homeware and tableware, as well as carpets, embroidery and towels.
tessanda.ch

DO

HAUSER & WIRTH
St Moritz
Contemporary, global and free-to-enter, the St Moritz iteration of Hauser & Wirth's empire spans three floors of the Palace Galerie in a space designed by Paris-based architect Luis Laplace.
hauserwirth.com

SCALA
St Moritz
For a cinematic experience steeped in history and culture, visit the sleek art deco-style film house that has been stirring its viewers for more than nine decades.
scala-stmoritz.ch

CRYSTAL PIANO BAR
St Moritz
Lovers of cocktails and the tinkling of soft piano keys need look no further. This piano bar, tucked inside the Crystal Hotel, is the perfect place for an après-ski apéro.
crystalhotel.ch

ATELIER BOLT
Klosters (Graubünden)
Sculptor and painter Christian Bolt has created a vibrant cultural hub in his beloved Klosters, turning a former cowshed into a space for his interdisciplinary work.
bolt.ch

BÜNDNER KUNSTMUSEUM
Chur (Graubünden)
An important 8,000-strong collection of Swiss and, in particular, local Graubündian art.
kunstmuseum.gr.ch

NORTH & NORTHEAST

Switzerland's northern reaches include French and German-speaking populations and a diverse landscape that spreads across the central plateau and the Jura mountains. It encompasses both isolated rural villages and small, prosperous cities such as Baden and St Gallen.

STAY

MAMMERTSBERG
Freidorf (Thurgau)
Mammertsberg offers a peaceful retreat in a historic villa. The hotel's terrace overlooks Lake Constance while the restaurant provides an avant-garde fine dining experience.
mammertsberg.ch

SCHLOSS WARTEGG
Rorschacherberg (St Gallen)
The hotel offers a peaceful stay in a historic castle, originally built in 1557. For a stroll among lush greenery visit its surrounding protected park.
wartegg.ch

HOTEL PORTO SOFIE
Gottlieben (Thurgau)
Offering individually furnished rooms adorned with elegant antiques, Hotel Porto Sofie reaps the benefits of its central location while maintaining an air of tranquillity.
portosofie.ch

HUUS LÖWEN
Gonten (Appenzell Innerrhoden)
A woody, fragrant wellness hotel. Have dinner in the cosy, ambient restaurant, then allow the exposed timber of its lofty rooms to facilitate a deeply quiet, restful slumber.
appenzellerhuus.ch

GRAND RESORT BAD RAGAZ
Bad Ragaz (St Gallen)
Grand Resort Bad Ragaz is best known for its iconic bathing hall warmed by a nearby hot spring, a traditional "bathing cure" that predates the rise in popularity of the ski resort as the predominant Swiss holiday pastime.
resortragaz.ch

Comfort inside and out at Rebstock

EAT & DRINK

REBSTOCK
Baden
Home to one of Baden's best summer terraces, Rebstock offers refined comfort food, an excellent local wine list and the joy of neighbourhood belonging.
rebstockbaden.ch

WILLI SCHMID
Lichtensteig (St Gallen)
Willi Schmid's fresh jersey blue and bergmatter are exclusively available here. And with a little luck, you can watch the cheesemaker at work through the window.
willischmid.ch

AESCHER
Weissbad (Appenzell Innerrhoden)
Tucked away in the mountains, this restaurant and guesthouse has welcomed hikers since 1860. Whether you're hopping on the cable car or taking the steep hike, local flavours await you.
aescher.ch

ZUM GOLDENEN SCHÄFLI
St Gallen
Enjoy a classic menu in St Gallen's last remaining guild house. Brimming with character, this convivial venue from 1484 is decked out with wood-panelled walls and sloped flooring.
zumgoldenenschaeflisg.ch

PFÄNDLER'S GASTHOF ZUM BÄREN
Birmenstorf (Aargau)
Inside this historic building, punters can opt to dine in a charming wood-panelled restaurant or an airy orangerie. In the summer months, be sure to venture outside into the garden for a sparkling aperitif.
zumbaeren.ch

DO

KIRCHGASSE
Steckborn (Thurgau)
The extraordinary gallery space in the beautifully restored 16th-century Haus zur Hoffnung building represents 11 artists across photography, sculpture and painting.
kirchgasse.com

ST MARTIN UND CALFEISENTAL
St Martin (St Gallen)
St Martin is an idyllic village nestled in a valley in the heart of a Unesco World Heritage Site. The area was first settled in the 14th century and its wooden houses set the scene for a peaceful day off the radar.
sankt-martin.ch

BASEL

Basel is Switzerland's third-largest city and has a history stretching back more than 2,000 years. It is considered the nation's culture capital, hosting one of the highest concentrations of museums per capita of any city in Europe, as well as the internationally famous Art Basel art fair.

STAY

HOTEL KRAFFT
Basel
In 1873 Swiss architect Ferdinand Iselin turned three medieval houses into a hotel. It spans five breathtaking floors and is steeped in history.
krafftbasel.ch

EAT & DRINK

CONSUM
Basel
A Barcelona-inspired wine bar that serves as Hotel Krafft's de facto canteen and as a hub for passers-by who want a good glass of wine in a casual atmosphere.
consumbasel.ch

CAFÉ FRÜHLING
Basel
Frühling has grown into a beloved local hub, offering a sun-soaked terrace on which to enjoy your morning coffee.
cafe-fruehling.ch

XOCOLATL
Basel
This much-loved chocolatier and confectioner experiments with international cocoa varieties, innovative recipes and a modern bean-to-bar philosophy.
xocolatl.ch

VOLKSHAUS
Basel
The brasserie serves up dishes merging Swiss home cooking with *cuisine du marché* and, come nightfall, the bar spills onto the pavement out front.
volkshaus-basel.ch

Von Bartha's striking spaces

SHOP

VIU
Basel
Since opening in 2013, Viu has taken Switzerland by storm using cutting-edge techniques to create its premium specs and shades.
shopviu.com

BLANCHE
Basel
Made by niche, mostly Swiss creators, the clothes at Blanche are characterised by their distinctive and individual designs.
blanchestudioshop.ch

GRIMSEL
Basel
Composed of carefully curated items and a thriving in-house line, Grimsel was opened by graphic designer Alexa Früh and interior architect Bettina Ginsberg in 2014.
grimsel.net

DO

FONDATION BEYELER
Riehen (Basel-Stadt)
More than 400 works of modern, contemporary and impressionist art occupy the building, which was designed by Renzo Piano.
fondationbeyeler.ch

VON BARTHA
Basel
Housed in two repurposed spaces – a reimagined garage in Basel and a lighthouse in Copenhagen – Von Bartha has been a force in modern and contemporary art since 1970.
vonbartha.com

SUDHAUS
Basel
Formerly an old brewery, Sudhaus is now a 400-capacity concert venue and party space that enlivens the city and shapes its nightlife.
sudhaus.ch

KUNSTMUSEUM BASEL
Basel
The Kunstmuseum Basel is home to the world's oldest public art collection. With more than 300,000 works spanning eight centuries, the museum's collection is vast and continues to grow.
kunstmuseumbasel.ch

BERNE & JURA

The cantons of Berne and Jura have a shared history stretching back many centuries. The city of Berne is the de facto national capital and is also capital of its canton, with a vibrant cultural life. The mostly French-speaking Jura voted to secede from predominantly German-speaking Berne in 1978.

STAY

CHÂTEAU DE RAYMONTPIERRE
Val Terbi (Jura)
This sixteenth-century building has retained its early modern charm, with shuttered windows, a protruding curved turret and a curtain wall.
chateauderaymontpierre.ch

BELLEVUE PALACE
Berne
This heritage-listed institution dating back to the belle époque era boasts historic chandeliers and neoclassical frescoes and was once a favourite of British novelist John le Carré.
bellevue-palace.ch

GRAND HOTEL BELVEDERE
Wengen (Berne, canton)
Combining tradition with sophisticated modernity, the 90 state-of-the-art rooms and suites, each with panoramic views, are designed to reflect their Alpine surroundings.
beaumier.com

YETI HUTS
Grindelwald (Berne, canton)
Seven idyllic, fully equipped huts that could be straight out of a *Heidi* film, complete with traditional, cosy furnishings.
yeti.ch

THE BRECON
Adelboden (Berne, canton)
First built in 1914, the Brecon is a chalet-inspired hotel with the charms of a Swiss timber cottage.
thebrecon.com

HOTEL OLDEN
Gstaad
The quintessentially Swiss façade of Hotel Olden belies its reputation as a bon vivant hangout in the 1970s.
hotelolden.com

A well-earned treat at Apfelgold

HOTEL GRIMSEL HOSPIZ
Guttannen (Berne, canton)
Built in 1934, the historic Alpine Hotel Grimsel's castle-like stone building – complete with bold red shutters – is an idyllic mountaintop outpost.
grimselwelt.ch

AUBERGE DU MOUTON
Porrentruy (Jura)
This 12-room figurehead hotel is a master work of stripped-back luxury, showcasing rustic elements of Swiss heritage, light modern touches and an ambient restaurant.
dumouton.ch

GSTAAD PALACE
Gstaad
One of the last family-owned Swiss luxury hotels, Gstaad Palace retains the Swiss chalet feel that has welcomed international royalty and aristocracy.
palace.ch

EAT & DRINK

DOMAINE BLATTNER
Soyhières (Jura)
Founded in 1991 by Silvia and Valentin Blattner, this charming farmhouse quickly became the perfect spot to enjoy a glass of wine with a unique origin.
domaineblattner.ch

CASA NOVO
Berne
Appealingly positioned above the River Aare overlooking a jumble of medieval riverside townhouses, Casa Novo's international menu homes in on produce from regional suppliers.
casa-novo.ch

APFELGOLD
Berne
At Apfelgold, you can taste some apple varieties as juice, cider, nonalcoholic spritz or purée. As for the baked goods, other seasonal fruit options are on offer too.
apfelgold.ch

RÖSSLI
Feutersoey-Gstaad (Berne, canton)
In winter, the wood-panelled dining rooms offers 40 seats. In summer, more seats are added under the fruit trees in the garden.
restaurantroessli.swiss

DREI BERGE
Mürren (Berne, canton)
Perched at 1,638 metres among sheer rock faces, Drei Berge is a 1907 forest-green building complete with red and white shutters – a spectacle in a spectacular place.
dreibergehotel.ch

MOLKEREI GSTAAD
Gstaad
Molkerei (meaning dairy) has been crafting exquisite Alpine cheese since 1931, courtesy of the town's longstanding heritage of mountain dairy farming.
molkerei-gstaad.ch

FIESCHERBLICK
Grindelwald (Berne, canton)
Hotel guests and those further afield are invited to Fiescherblick in the mornings for breakfast classics and excellent coffee, and later in the day for seasonal dishes made with regional produce.
hotel-fiescherblick.ch

CONFISERIE TSCHIRREN
Berne
Nearly a century old, Confiserie Tschirren has been synonymous with first-class Swiss confectionery for three generations.
swiss-chocolate.ch

LE SOLEIL DE CHÂTILLON
Châtillon (Jura)
Creating a relaxed and convivial ambience, this restaurant intertwines gastronomy and nature with a lush green terrace space, herbarium and a flavourful menu.
lesoleildechatillon.ch

SHOP

MAISON LORENZ BACH
Gstaad
Alongside the big players, at the Lorenz Bach boutique you'll also find a goldmine of over 150 hard-to-find labels.
lorenzbach.ch

STOOR
Berne
Combining high-quality, eco-conscious materials and timeless aesthetics, Stoor produces sustainable garments and accessories using modern and elegant designs.
stoor.ch

USM
Berne
The Swiss-manufactured furniture company is in fine form here. Much like the modular pieces on offer, the displays change regularly – visitors enter at risk of planning an entire home makeover using their innovative pieces.
usm.com

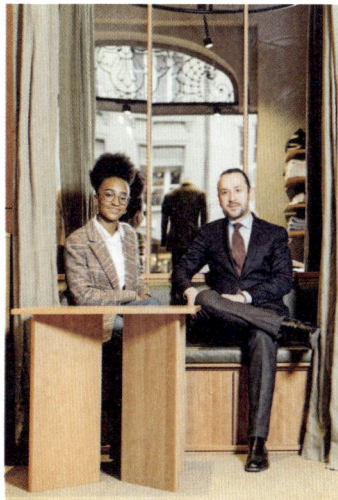

Measure up at Pelikamo

ZWAHLEN-HÜNI
Saanen (Berne, canton)
Alongside their tailoring service, this multi-brand boutique offers German and Austrian traditional costumes, a range of clothing and premium leather shoes.
zwahlenhueni.ch

MAGGS
Berne
A fashion and lifestyle concept store that hosts an attractive selection of labels including Isabel Marant and Ganni, as well as a selection of second-hand, high-end fashion.
maggs.ch

KITCHENER
Berne
Brands such as Toast, Maska, APC and home-bred label Kitchener Items are shown across this 680 sq m space, which also displays premium homeware and pantry supplies.
shop.kitchener.ch

PELIKAMO
Berne
Menswear brand Pelikamo dresses bankers day and night via its bespoke suiting service, as well as offering a more casual collection for everyday wear.
pelikamo.com

DO

ZENTRUM PAUL KLEE
Berne
For the ultimate cultural fix, head to the Zentrum Paul Klee: this interdisciplinary cultural centre features 4,000 works by the Swiss-German artist and often showcases other masters.
zpk.org

BUCHHANDLUNG ZUM ZYTGLOGGE
Berne
Founded in 1936, this bookshop attracts passers-by with traditional charm and thoughtfully arranged shelves. Visitors will find books on the local region as well as from further afield.
zytglogge-buchhandlung.ch

EINSTEIN HAUS
Berne
Now a humble museum space, the former residence of Albert Einstein tells the story of the illustrious physicist and his pioneering discoveries during his time in Berne.
einstein-bern.ch

SWITZERLAND
The MONOCLE Handbook

ACKNOWLEDGEMENTS

MONOCLE

Editorial Director & Chairman
Tyler Brûlé

Editor in Chief
Andrew Tuck

Creative Director
Richard Spencer Powell

Production Director
Jacqueline Deacon

Photography Director
Matthew Beaman

Art Director
Sam Brogan

SWITZERLAND: THE MONOCLE HANDBOOK

Head of Book Publishing
Virginia McLeod

Editor
Amy van den Berg

Deputy Editors
Josh Lee
Aimee Dexter

Designers
Jessica North-Lewis
Carey Alborough

Photography Editor
Sara Taglioretti

Production Coordinator
Marta Fernàndez Canut

Sub Editor
Matt Dupuy

Writer
Claudia Jacob

ILLUSTRATORS

Owen Gatley
Matteo Riva
Nikolai Senin & Natalia Senina

SPECIAL THANKS

Alexandra Aldea
Virgiliu Andone
Desiree Bandli
Vanessa Bird
Rob Gibson
Beth Mason
Conor McCann
Amy Richardson
Alex de Royere
Carlo Silberschmidt
Zayana Zulkiflee

WRITERS

Desiree Bandli
Amy van den Berg
Jessica Bridger
Gabe Bullard
Christina Hubbeling
Rory Jones
Helena Kardová
Chloé Lake
Julia Lasica
Virginia McLeod
Ilona Marx
Emily Rose Mawson
Sophie Monaghan-Coombs
Lucrezia Motta
Marcela Palek
Maria Papakleantous
Anton Preuss
Stella Roos
Laura Rysman
Marie-Sophie Schwarzer
Brenda Tuohy
Kaira van Wijk
Valentina Venelli
Emilie Wade
Sonia Zhuravlyova
Myriam Zumbuehl

PRINCIPAL PHOTOGRAPHERS

Andrea Pugiotto
Romain Mader
Guillaume Megevand
Sabine Hess
Samuel Schalch

PHOTOGRAPHERS

Yves Bachmann
Martin Brusewitz
Jamani Caillet
Paul Clemence
Fabrizio D'Aloisio
Giacomo Demelli
Jonathan Ducrest
Marc Ducrest
Thomas Egli
Leo Fabrizio
Selina Feuerstein
Luigi Fiano
Noë Flum
Johannes Fredheim
Philip Frowein
Catherine Gailloud
Antoine Georgelin
Bea De Giacomo
Chiara Goia
Nils Grubba
Maurice Haas
Ramon Haindl
Philipp Hänger
Ariel Huber
Joel Hunn
Rafael Palacio Illingworth
Jessica Jungbauer
Katya Kalyska
Younes Klouche
Mirjam Kluka
Kensington Leverne
Katharina Lütscher
Consiglio Manni
Lea Meienberg
Joan Minder
Anne Morgenstern
Martin Morrell
Dylan Perrenoud
Thomas Prior
Lea Reutimann
Robert Rieger
Steivan Schlegel
Melody Sky
Horatiu Sovaiala
Benjamin Swanson
Clara Tuma
Karla Hiraldo Voleau
Annik Wetter
David Willen and Tania Willen
Samuel Zeller
Marvin Zilm
Andreas Zimmermann
Jürg Zimmermann

IMAGE LIBRARIES

Alamy
Freezinglightstudio
Getty Images
Shutterstock

Join our club

In 2007, MONOCLE was launched as a monthly magazine briefing on global affairs, business, design and more. Today we have a thriving print business, a radio station, shops, cafés, books, films and events. At our core is the simple belief that there will always be a place for a brand that is committed to telling fresh stories, delivering good journalism and being on the ground around the world. We're Zürich and London-based and have bureaux in Hong Kong, Paris and Tokyo. Subscribe at *monocle.com*.

Monocle magazine

MONOCLE is published 10 times a year, including two double issues (July/August and December/ January). We also have annual specials: THE FORECAST, THE ENTREPRENEURS and THE ESCAPIST. Look out for our seasonal newspapers too.

Monocle Radio

Our round-the-clock online radio station delivers global news and shows covering foreign affairs, urbanism, business, culture, food and drink, design and print media. You can listen live or download shows from *monocle.com/radio* — or wherever you get your podcasts.

Books

Since 2013, MONOCLE has been publishing books such as this one, covering a range of topics from home design to how to live a gentler life. Also available in this series are Handbooks for Portugal, Spain, France and Greece. All our books are available on our website, through our distributor, Thames & Hudson, or at all good bookshops.

Monocle Minute

MONOCLE's smartly appointed family of newsletters comes from our team of editors and bureau chiefs around the world. From the daily *Monocle Minute* to *The Monocle Weekend Editions* and our weekly *Monocle On Design* special, sign up to get the latest in affairs, entrepreneurship and design, straight to your inbox every day — all for free. *monocle.com/minute*

MONOCLE